Violent Legacies

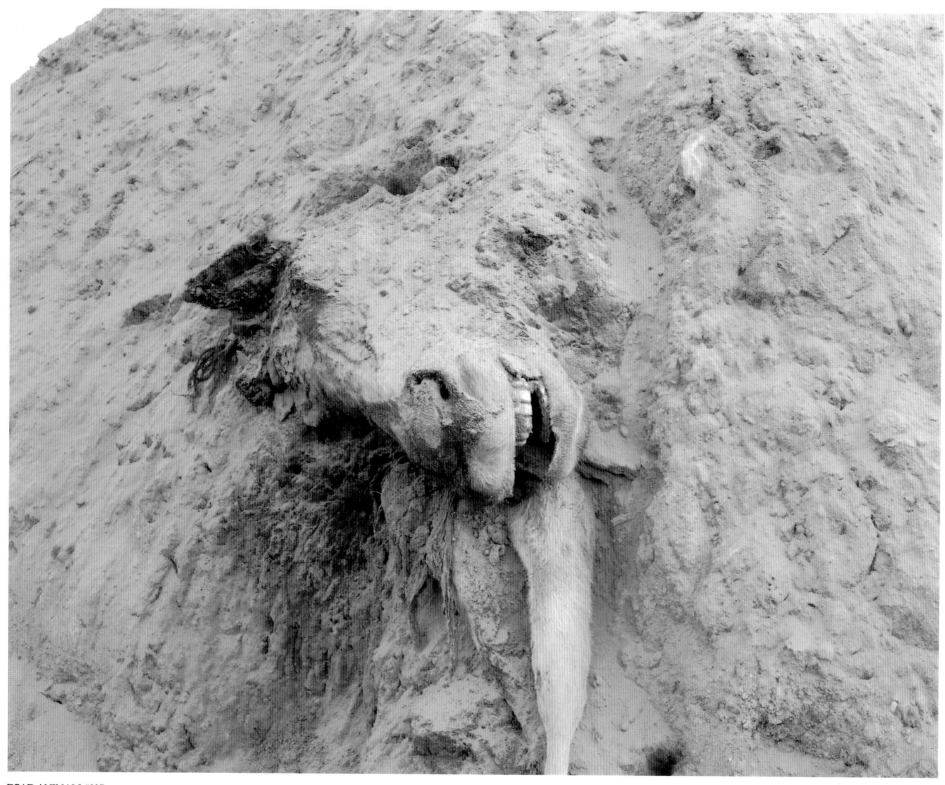

DEAD ANIMALS #327

Violent Legacies

three cantos

BY RICHARD MISRACH

FICTION BY
SUSAN SONTAG

APERTURE

This book is dedicated to my mother and father.

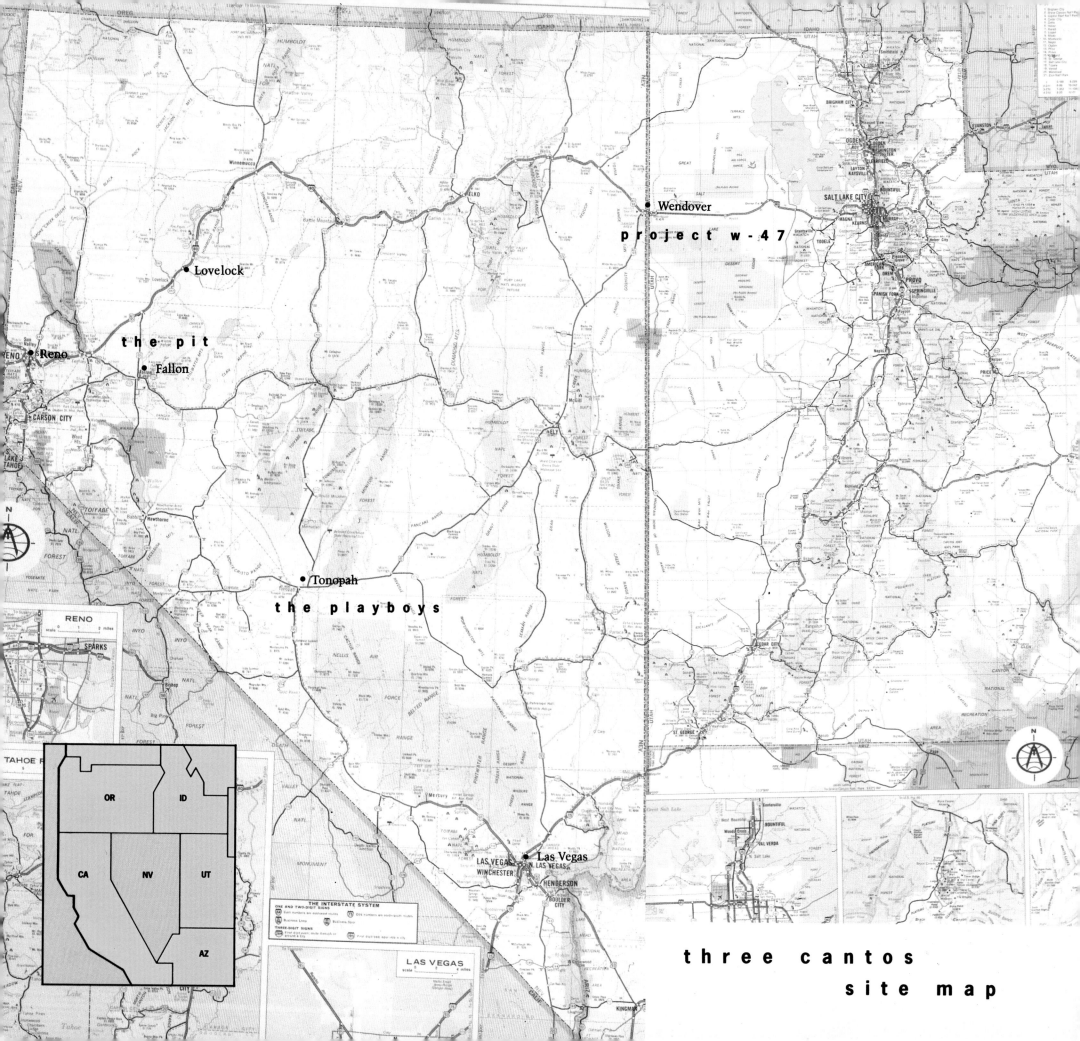

Wendover

project w-47

the pit

Reno

Lovelock

Fallon

Tonopah

the playboys

Las Vegas

**three cantos
site map**

contents

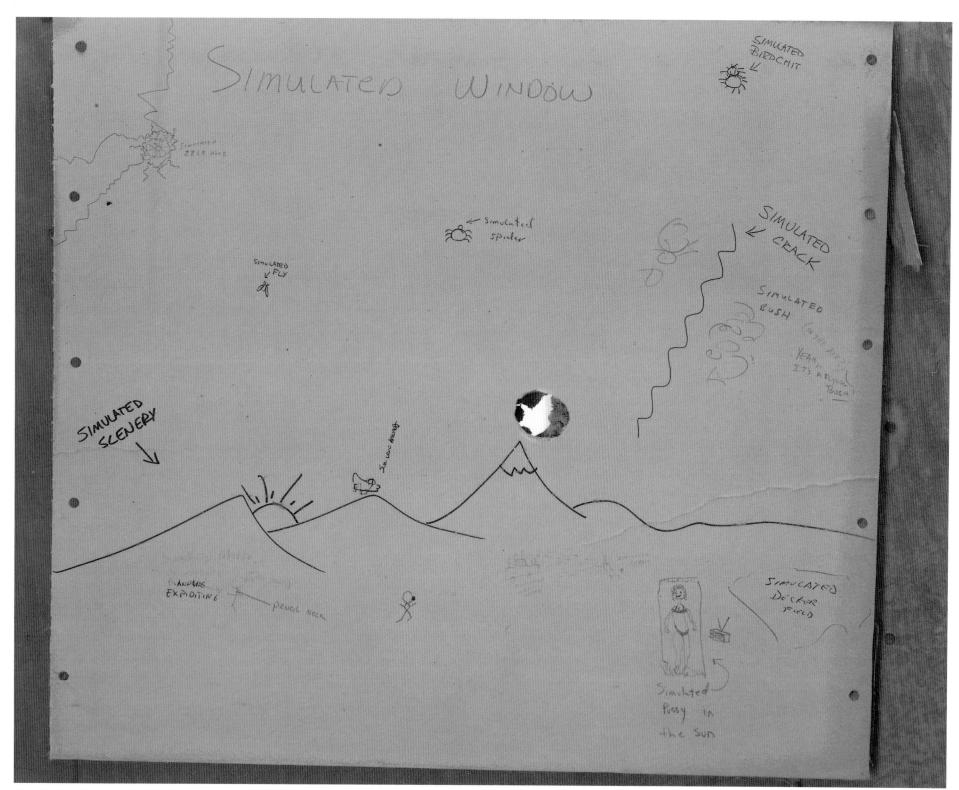

simulated window GRAFFITI, HANGAR OF THE *ENOLA GAY* Wendover Air Base, Utah, 1986

the view from the ark
by susan sontag

"Tell me a story," said one of the descendants of Noah. "Yes, tell me a story."

"What kind of story? Hmm. I can tell you a story with a happy ending."

"Don't condescend to me. I can take it. Just tell a story."

"Then I'll tell a story with an unhappy ending. But after a while you'll stop paying attention. I'll see you fidgeting, your gaze wandering. And I'll ask you what's wrong and you'll tell me you've heard this story already. You'll say it didn't have to turn out so badly."

"Are there only two kinds of stories? I don't believe you!"

"The sky is wide, oh. The sea is deep, oh. And all the stories have been told, oh. Oh. Oh. Oh."

"Stop! You're just trying to frighten me. But it's no use, no use trying to frighten me. I have to keep my spirits up. I knew you were a gloombird. You *like* frightening me."

"Me, gloomy? How wrong you are. I love being alive. Swooping, darting, alighting wherever I want. It's just that if I look around me, I can't help feeling discouraged."

"Listen, you're supposed to be a bringer of good news."

"I can only report what I see."

"Well, fly away then. And don't come back until you have something optimistic to report."

"You see, I told you, you didn't want to hear any bad news."

"Well, I don't like hearing bad news all the time. Can you blame me?"

"Okay, I'll try again. Don't think I like being a calamitist, I don't. Now you hold tight and let me take another look."

"Hey, wait."

"What?"

"Don't get distracted out there. I mean, don't fool around. I mean, just bring back the news."

"First you berate me for being gloomy, then you mind my having a good time. But I can't help it. I was made for ecstasy. I'm an artist, you know."

"So where's the ecstasy?"

"Everywhere."

"Lucky you."

"Have you never known ecstasy?"

"Sure, but..."

"Right, I know. But then something brings you down. You're saddled with all these possessions you care about and have to take care of and replace, and all your big plans, and your relatives..."

"Lay off my relatives, you hear? They're doing the best they can."

"You're all doing the best you can. And part of that is ignoring the bad news until it comes and sits in your lap."

"Well, why shouldn't we be hopeful? Look at all we've already survived. And we're still here. We'll go on surviving. I know it."

"I hope so. I really hope you're right. Anyway, I'm outta here."

"But you're coming back?"

"Sure."

"Promise?"

"Of course, I'll be back."

• • • •

"Well, you took your time!"

"Sorry. I was enjoying myself."

"Anything else?"

"I was looking for some good news."

"And...?"

"Well, there's always some good news, if that's what you want to hear. Please don't think I enjoy worrying you."

"Go on, worry me."

"It really doesn't look so good out there. I saw some pretty appalling things."

"I bet you went out of your way to look for them."

"You don't have to look far."

"Maybe they don't look good to you. Maybe I would have another view."

"Okay, you try. I have some pictures."

"Oh, pictures. Great!"

"Take a look."

"Good Lord, it's the moon! The waters came down and we landed on the moon. Praise the Lord."

"No, it's the desert."

"Oh. Say, these are incredible."

"Thanks."

"It looks beautiful to me. All those golds and pinks and browns. And the sky. And the light. I don't see the problem."

"Well, it isn't just about seeing. You have to know

what's been going on. There's a story that goes with the pictures. When you know the story, the pictures mean something else."

"I know, now you're going to tell me about human wickedness. I've heard that story. That's why the flood came."

"No, I don't want to tell about anything so general. It's more about passivity. And power. You may notice that there aren't any people in the pictures. But this is what people have done."

"I still say, it looks beautiful to me."

"Sometimes when things are destroyed they look beautiful."

"*More* beautiful?"

"Sometimes."

"So how can you tell?"

"You have to know how to read the signs."

"Oh, that's just bird-talk."

"And people-talk, I assure you."

"Do a lot of people know this story?"

"A few. Actually quite a few. The question is not knowing, but caring."

"Well, you have to admit there's a lot to care about.

You can't care about everything."

"I think you ought to care about this."

"But the world is a very big place, isn't it. I mean, there's lots of room. Does it really matter what happens in a few places. If a few places get spoiled, or ruined, or defiled. There's always room to move on."

"You must be an American."

"A what?"

"Oh, never mind."

"I think I'll try this story out on a few people. Can I show them the pictures?"

"Sure..."

• • • •

"What did they say?"

"They said the pictures were beautiful."

"Nothing else?"

"They said they were worried, too."

"Anything else?"

"They said that there was nothing to be done."

"They said *that*? All of them?"

"Well, not all."

"And...?"

"They said it's a cruel world out there."

"Well, I'd say it's a cruel world in here, too. In your, what do you call it, Ark."

"We manage."

"Uh-huh."

"No, really! We just, you know, have to lower our expectations."

"As things get worse."

"Exactly."

"Who's being pessimistic now?"

"That's not pessimism. I call it realism."

"Oh, sure."

"And they also said to take what you've been telling me with a grain of salt. They said you were an artist."

"I already told you that."

"I thought your job was bringing news."

"Artists do that, too."

"Yeah, bad news."

"Not always, I assure you."

"They said that artists love to zero in on disasters. That they revel in bad news. And that artists are naïve moralists, who don't understand the iron laws of history. And, don't laugh, progress."

"Such as..."

"Well, why they have to do that. The people who run things. In the desert. The American desert. What you showed me in the pictures."

"So why. You tell me."

"It's because we have enemies. We have to be prepared. We have to defend ourselves."

"Parrot!"

"Hey, we're not all birds around here."

"You really believe what you just said?"

"Look, I'm taking in what you're telling me. It's really a shame. The animals and everything. But there are lots of other considerations, scientific, political, economic, that you wouldn't understand. You're a rover. You're an artist."

"Yeah. No ties. Free as a bird."

"Sort of."

"I can see you've met a lot of artists."

"I'm sorry if I've insulted you."

"Lord, Lord, give me strength! Oh, what fools these —"

"Don't squawk at me. I didn't do it. I didn't kill the animals. I didn't devastate the desert. I didn't rejoice in pumping pictures of sexy women with bullets. I didn't make Desert Storm."

"Did you know that porno films were screened for pilots in the Gulf War just before they were sent off on their bombing missions."

"American pilots."

"That's right."

"Listen, that's been common practice in more American colonial wars than I can count. But Americans didn't invent the link between testosterone and the pleasure of killing, especially killing defenseless people on the ground from high up in the air, any more than America is the only country poisoning its own lands. Listen to this, from a clipping someone gave me after looking at your pictures. 'I've never seen such colors. Nature doesn't have such colors. Twenty-five days later we went back to the village. The village was covered with dead animals, cats, dogs. We children dug a hole and buried them.' Guess who said that."

"Who?"

"A Kazakh writer who, in 1953, at the age of seven, watched the Soviet Union's first hydrogen-bomb test from a mountaintop a few miles from home."

"What are you trying to say?"

"That everybody does it. So why do you pick on America?"

"I guess I must be an American artist."

"Are you being sarcastic?"

"Me?"

"Yes, you."

"Solemn, earnest me?"

"Yes, you."

"So long, I'm off to the desert of cheerfulness."

"You know, admit it before you go, that violence is what nature is about."

"And human nature."

"Yes. Though not everyone behaves as badly as people can behave."

"Don't make it sound so perennial. This is happening now."

"Well, I'm not one of the perpetrators. The people who actually do these things wouldn't even talk to a being like you. People who do these things would just pick up a gun and blow you out of the sky."

Sound of flapping wings.

"Hey! Don't go! I'm not one of the Rulers of the Planet! I'm just a poor creature like you! Don't...go."

. . . .

"Here I am again."

Silence.

"Hello?"

"I thought you weren't coming back."

"Oh, I'm a persistent bird."

"You sure are! But, seriously, I admire you for not having given up."

"I figure if I keep on singing, it might sink in one day."

"Well, tenacity is one of the virtues. And the pictures are beautiful. Your catastrophe-landscapes. You don't mind if I tell you again how beautiful they are, do you?"

"Of course not, as long as you don't forget what they are about."

"I don't. I mean, I can't."

"But you'd like to forget what I've shown you, wouldn't you?"

"Sure I would. Who wants to feel more helpless?"

"But you won't forget."

"Even if I went blind, I couldn't forget these pictures."

"Funny that you should mention going blind. Because that's the theme of a homily I was intending to deliver to you. Ready for a homily?"

"Fire away."

"Oh, Lord."

"C'mon, can't you take a joke?"

"There are no jokes."

"You have to have a sense of humor. That's part of surviving."

Silence.

"Okay, okay."

Silence.

"Really, I'm listening."

"My homily. As you may or may not know, there are two kinds of blindness. Retinal blindness, which causes the eyes to deteriorate, and cortical blindness, resulting from a lesion in the brain, which leaves the eyes intact."

"How interesting."

"The point is that people who are cortically blind do in a sense see, that is, they are receiving visual impressions in consciousness. But they experience themselves as blind because these impressions don't pass into the much smaller arena of awareness. This has been demonstrated by a recent experiment."

"I like experiments."

"Yeah, I know. Well, anyway, you take someone who is cortically blind on one side, it could be the right. Seat that person at a table. Turn the person's head to the left. Then put some objects, say a coffee mug and a candlestick, on the right side of the table. If you ask, What do you see on the right side of the table, the answer is: Nothing. You know I'm blind on that side. But if you reply, Yes, that's correct, you can't see on that side, you're blind. But supposing you could see, let's just imagine that you could see, where would you guess the objects on the table are? And then, lo and behold, with only the slightest hesitation, the blind person extends her arm, opening her hand just a little for the slim candlestick, opening it wide for the fat mug."

"Wow! Is that a fact?"

"Yes. But this is a story. You asked me for a story. This is a parable."

"Whose meaning is...?"

"That it's the same with our actions. Just as we know so much more than we're aware of knowing, we can do much more than we believe ourselves capable of doing. Ask the direct question: What can we do about the destruction of the earth and the rising tide of human violence? The answer has to be: Nothing. Humans against animals, men against women, history against nature? Nothing. But what if we say, Right, nothing can be done. Nevertheless, if we imagine, just as a hypothesis, though clearly it's impossible..."

"I see," said Noah's descendant.

"Yes," said the bird. "Another frame for the will. For it's as plain as day, or night: the forests are being slain, the waters are being poisoned, the air is darkening and becoming noxious. Right, the world cannot be saved. But what if we acted anyway as if the world could be saved? Why then—"

"I see," repeated Noah's descendant.

"Yes," said the gloomy bird, brightening a little. "It is just barely possible that the world will be saved."

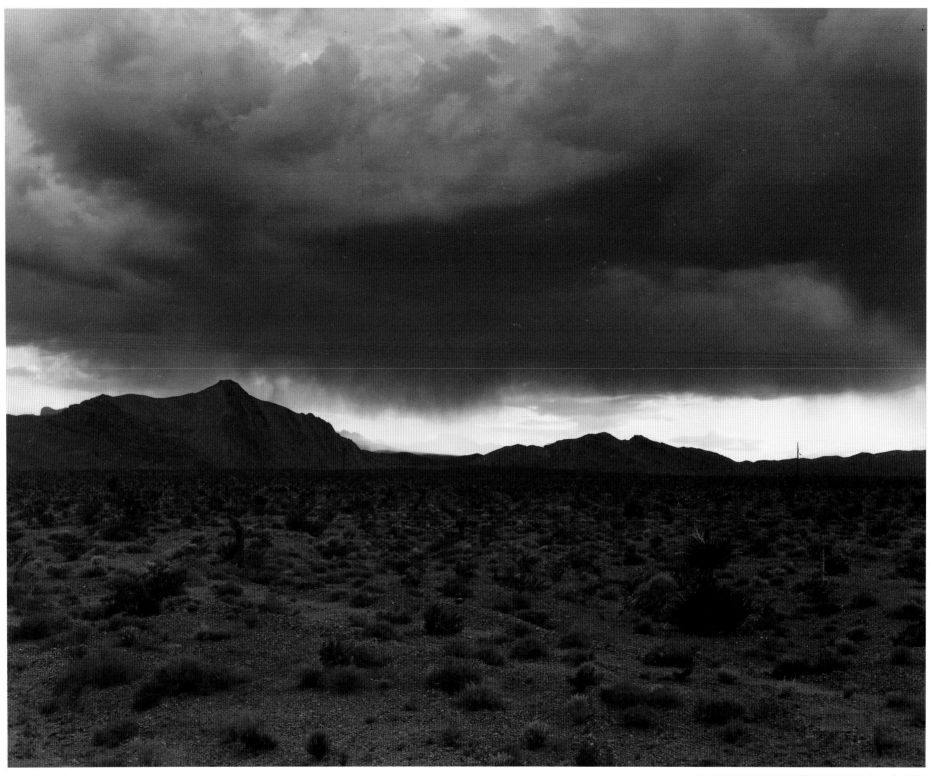

CLOUDBURST, NUCLEAR TEST SITE, Nevada, 1987

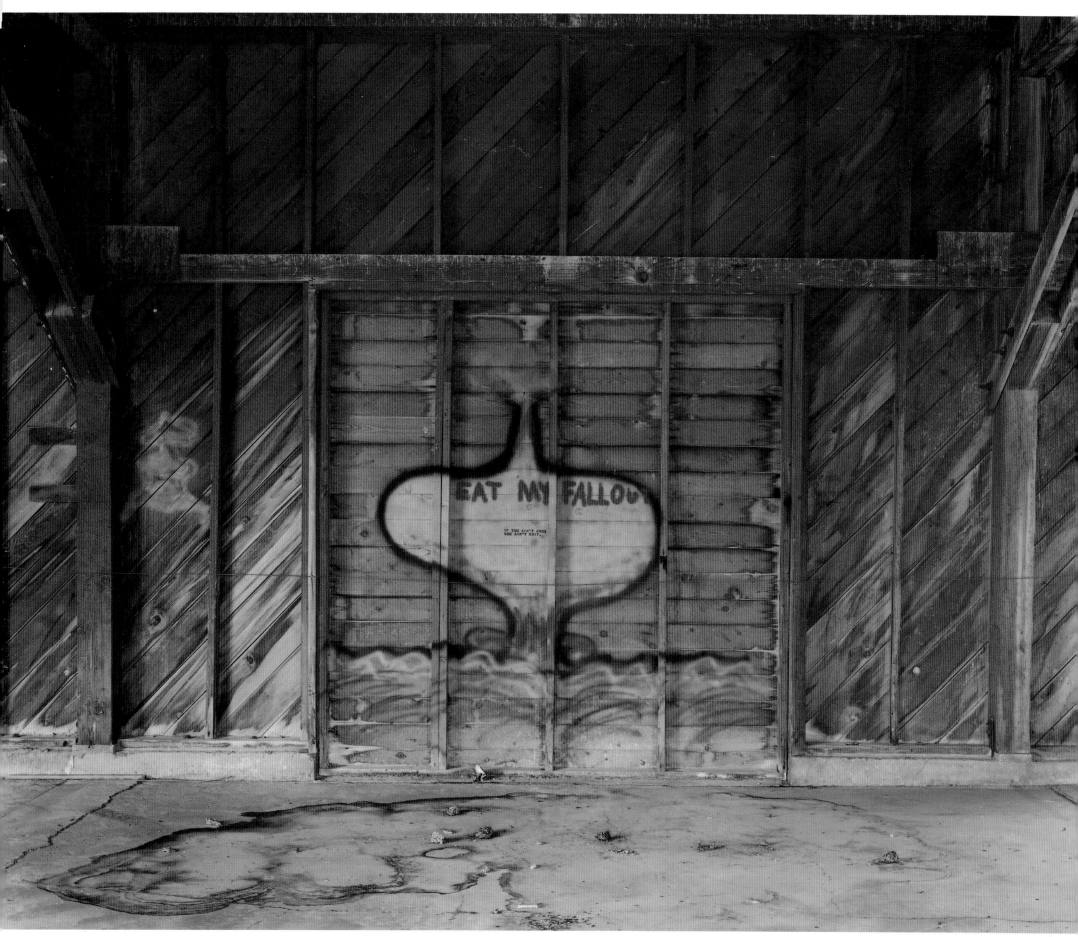

eat my fallout GRAFFITI, PROJECT W-47 ADMINISTRATIVE AND TECH-BUILDING

project w-47
(the secret)

Wendover Air Base, Utah (May – July 1945)

The final stages of the development of the atomic bomb were conducted in a remote, sparsely populated region of western Utah. It was here that previously researched and designed bomb components were modified, assembled, and flight-tested for the Hiroshima and Nagasaki bombings. The details of W-47 remain classified, and most military and government officials deny the project's existence.

(The "Project W-47" photographs were taken between 1986 and 1991)

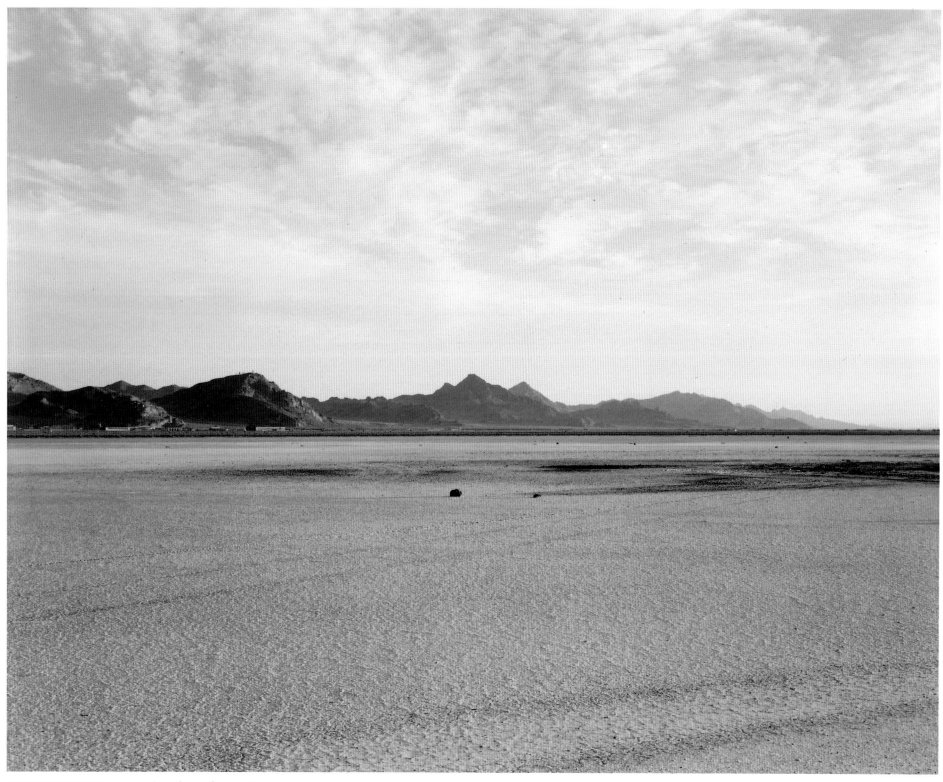

WENDOVER AIR BASE, view northeast from ordnance area

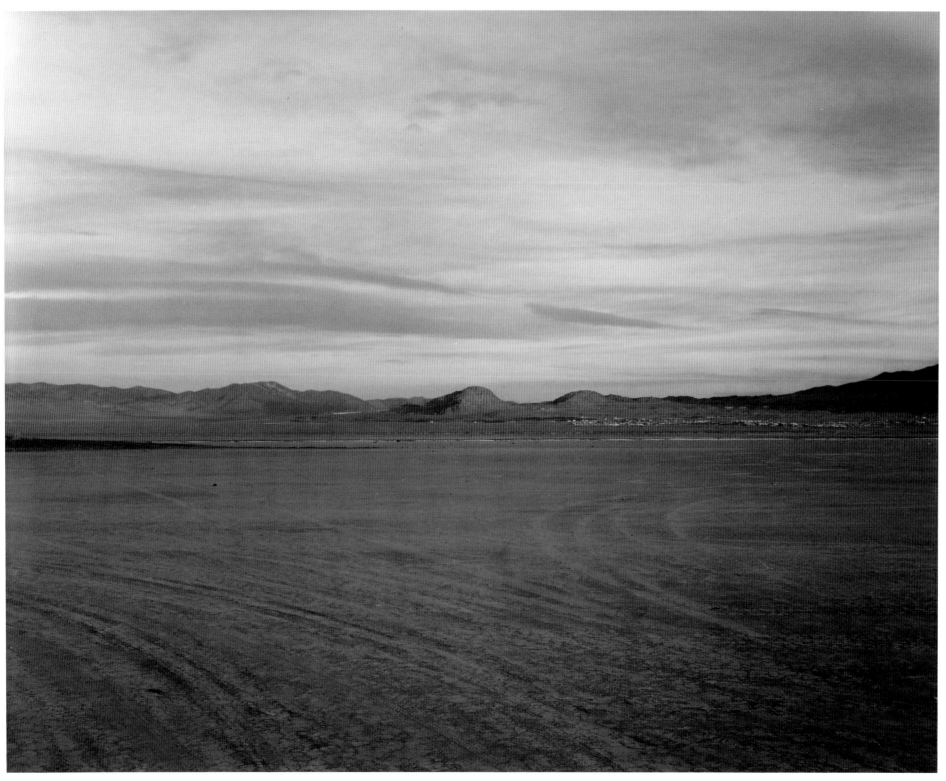

WENDOVER AIR BASE, view northwest from ordnance area

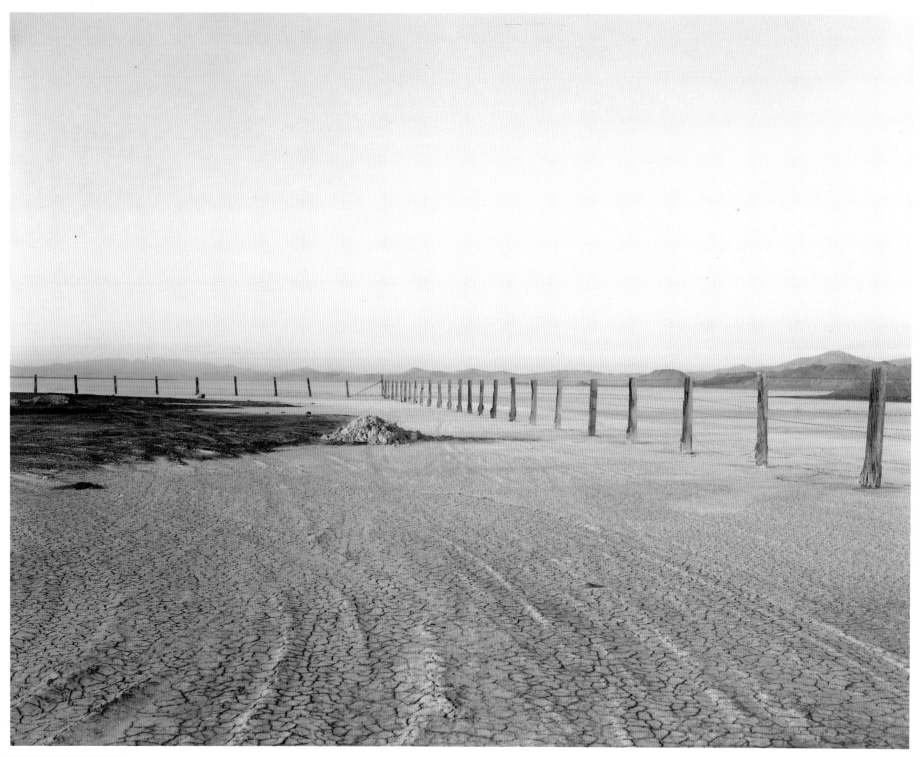

FENCING OF ORDNANCE AREA

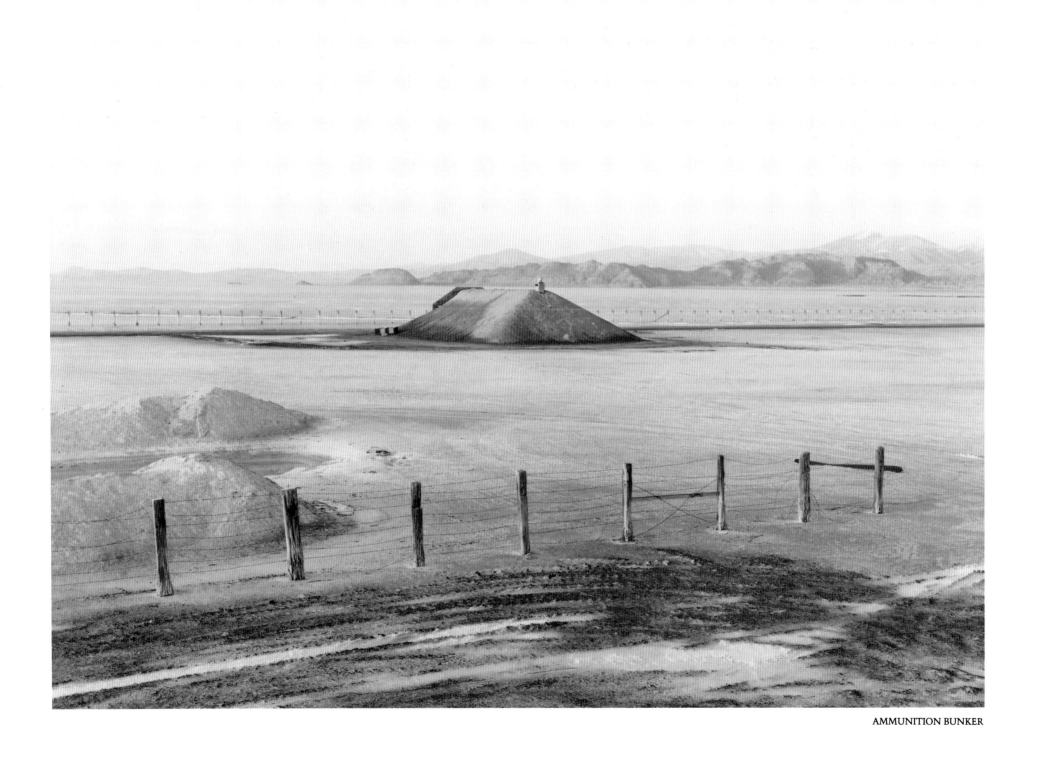

AMMUNITION BUNKER

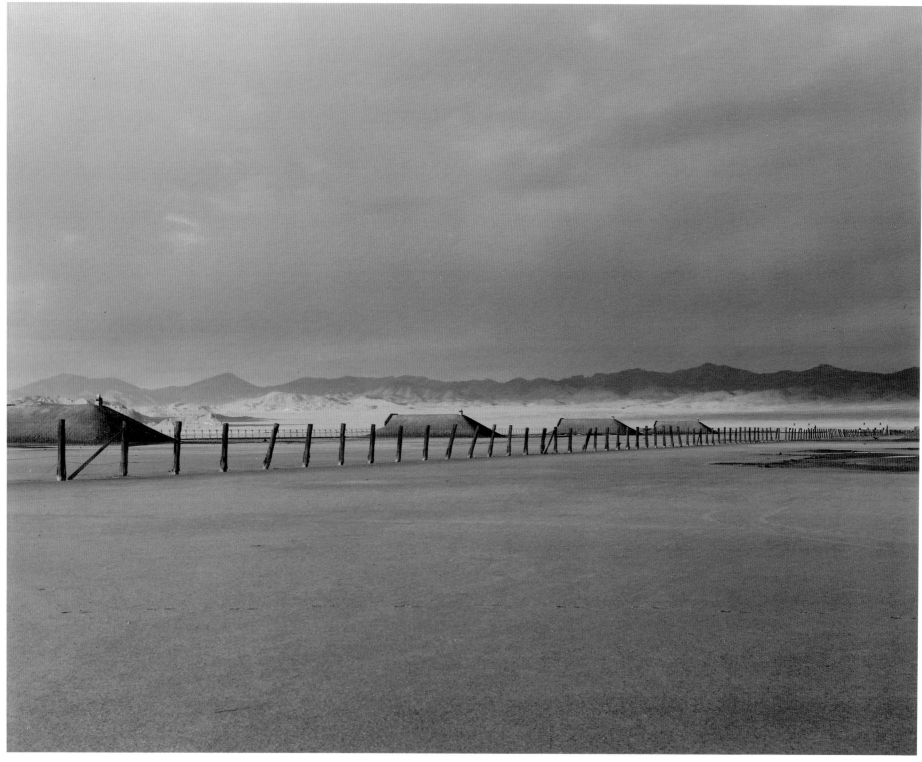

AMMUNITION BUNKERS

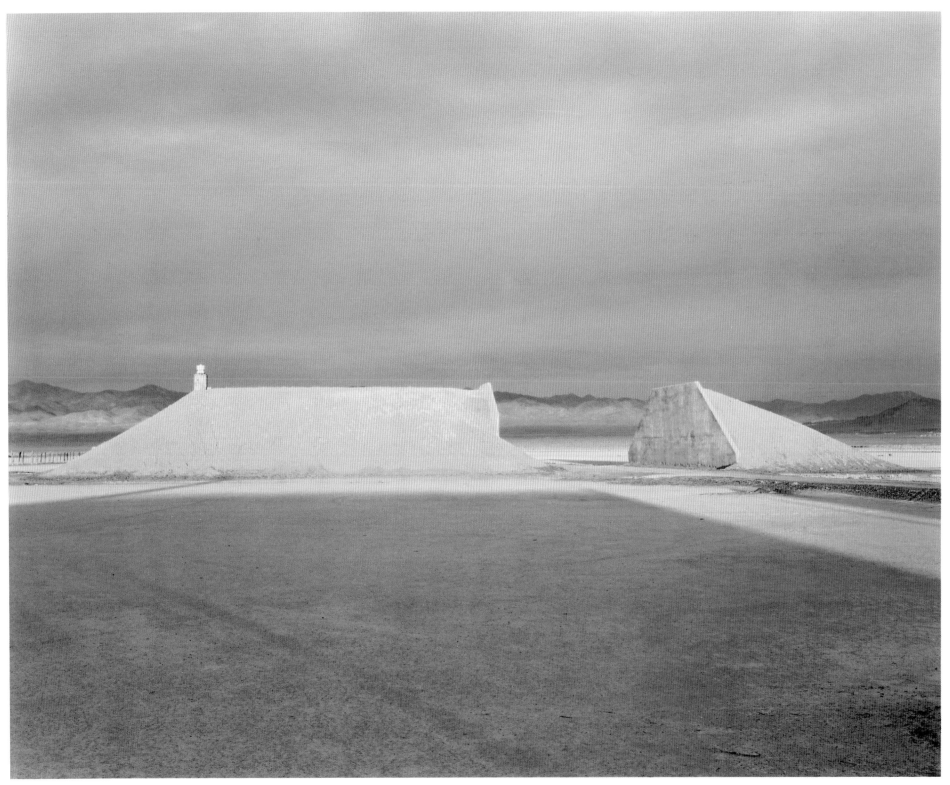

AMMUNITION BUNKER

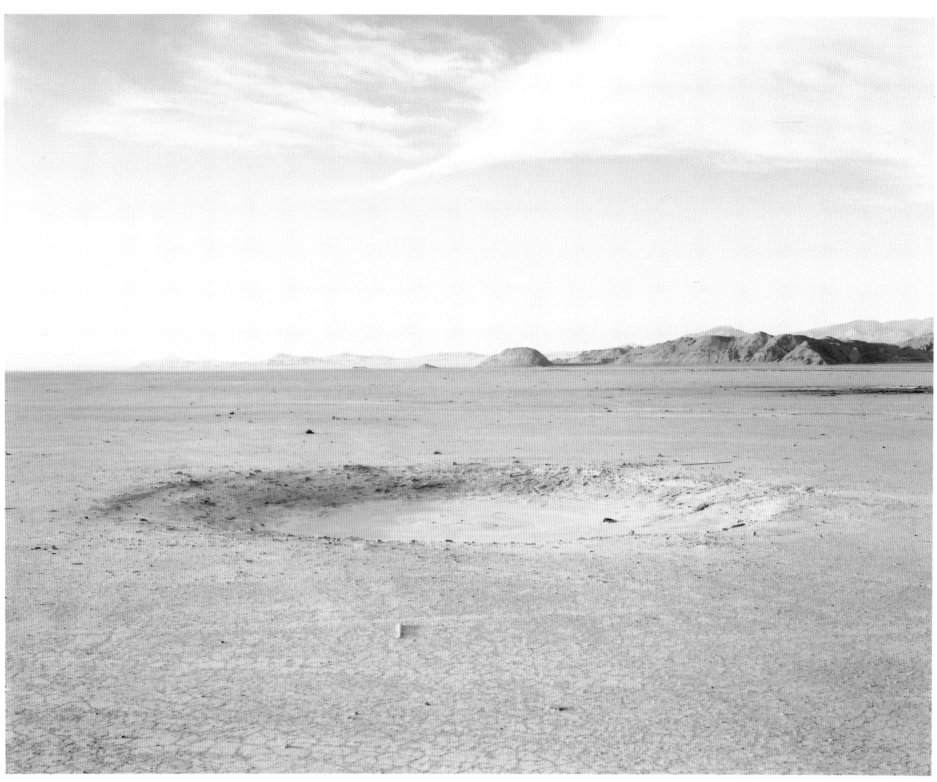

DETONATION CRATER

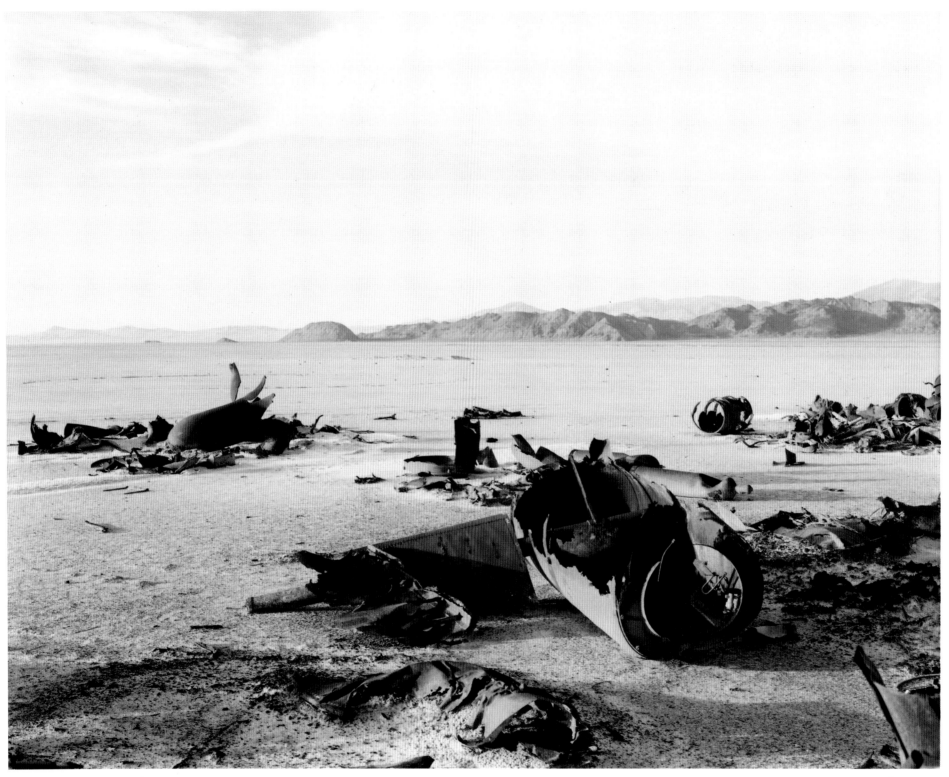

SHRAPNEL

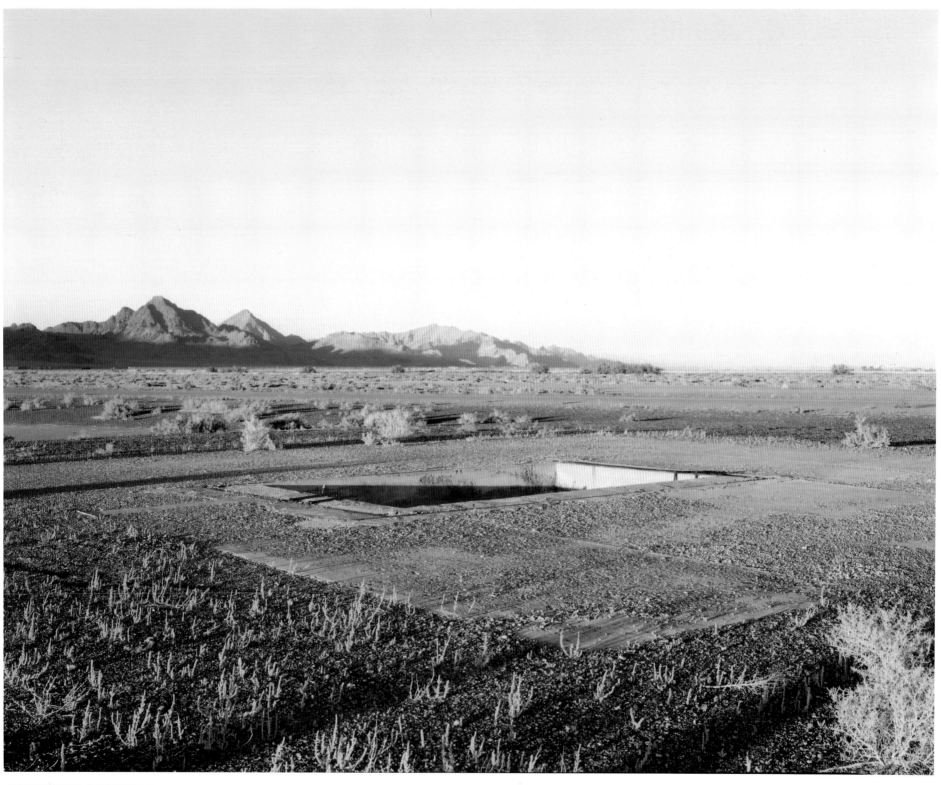

ATOMIC BOMB LOADING PIT #1

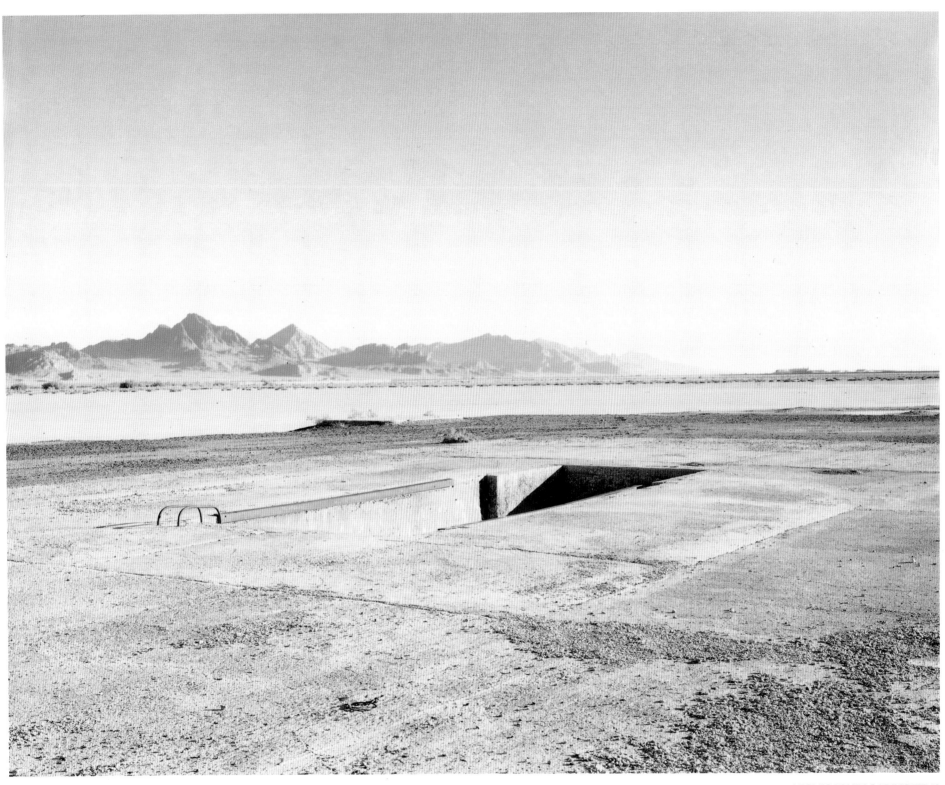

ATOMIC BOMB LOADING PIT #2

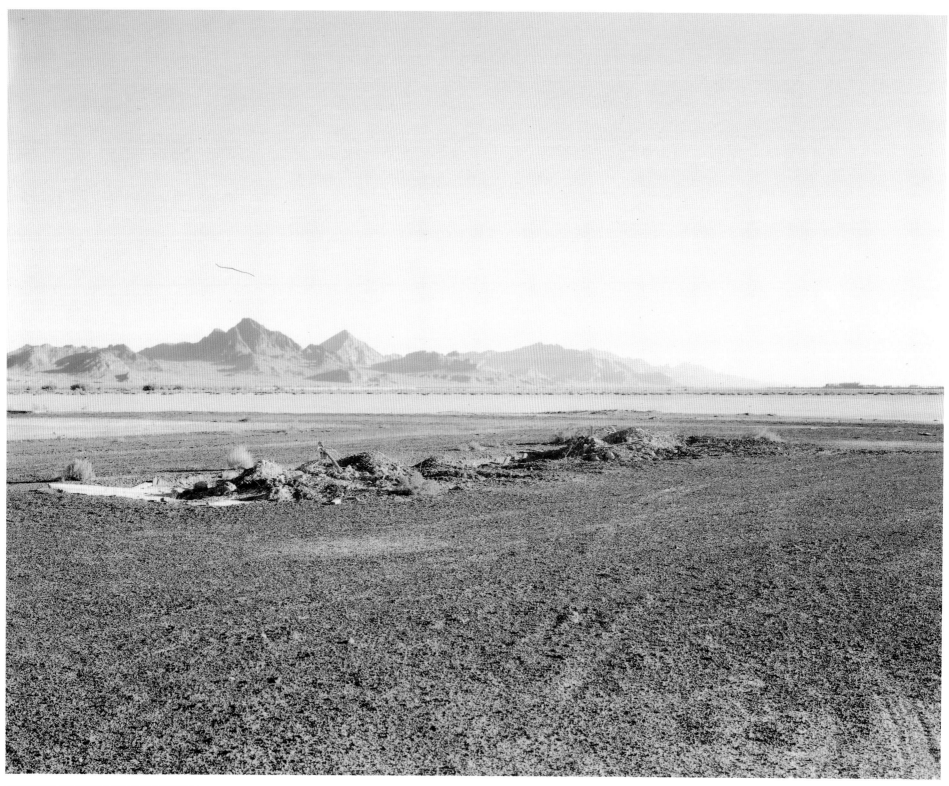

FIRST TEMPORARY LOADING PIT (DIRT)

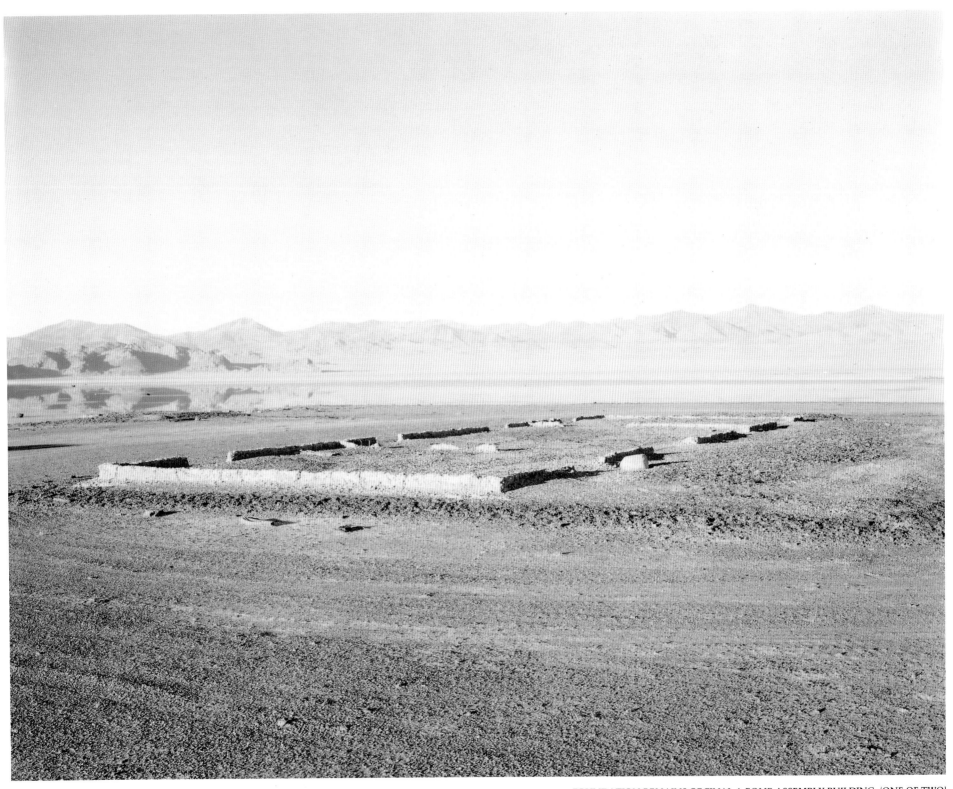

FOUNDATION REMAINS OF FINAL A-BOMB ASSEMBLY BUILDING (ONE OF TWO)

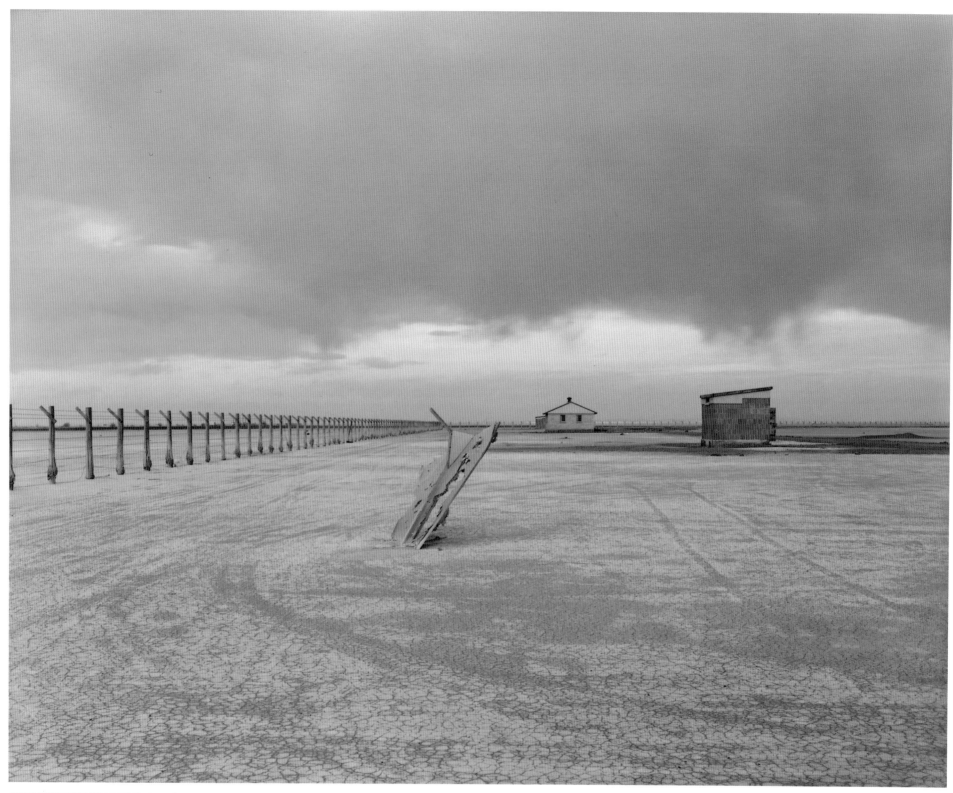

AERIAL TARGET ("DART") SHOT DOWN IN ORDNANCE AREA

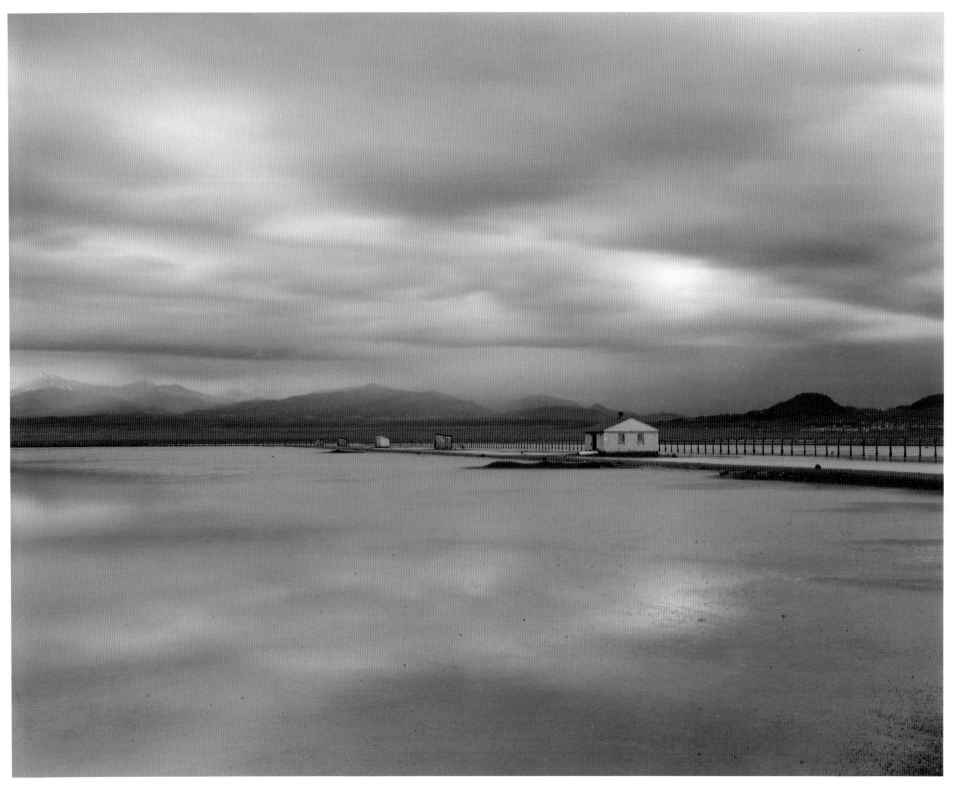

CHEMICAL BOMB AND PYROTECHNIC STORAGE

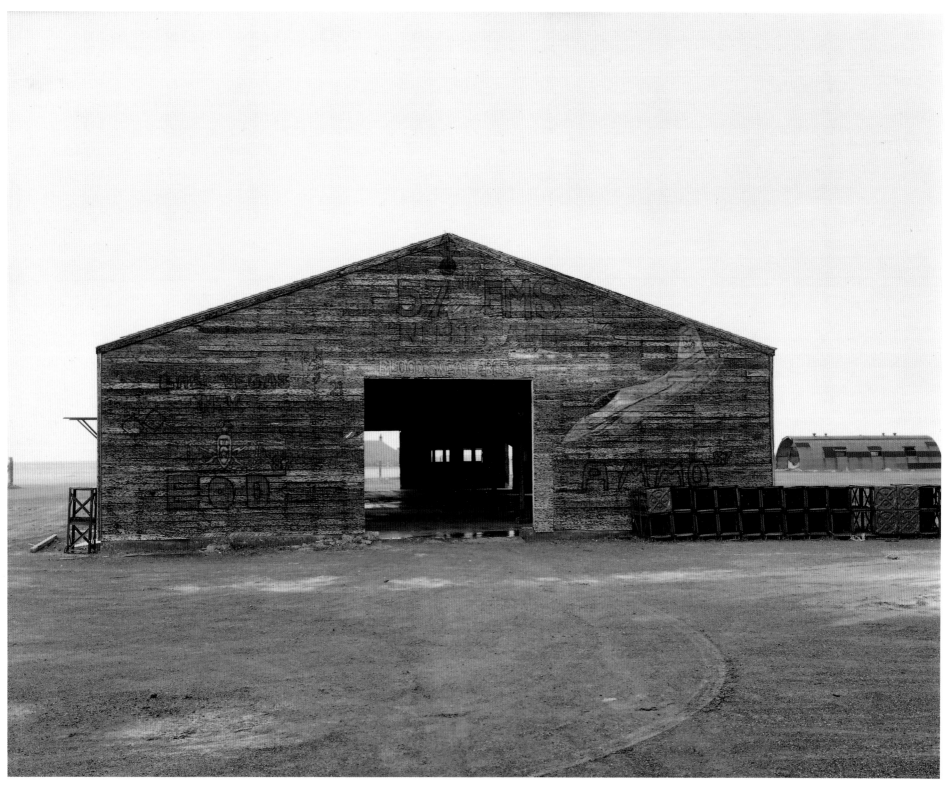

A-BOMB ASSEMBLY AND TESTING BUILDING

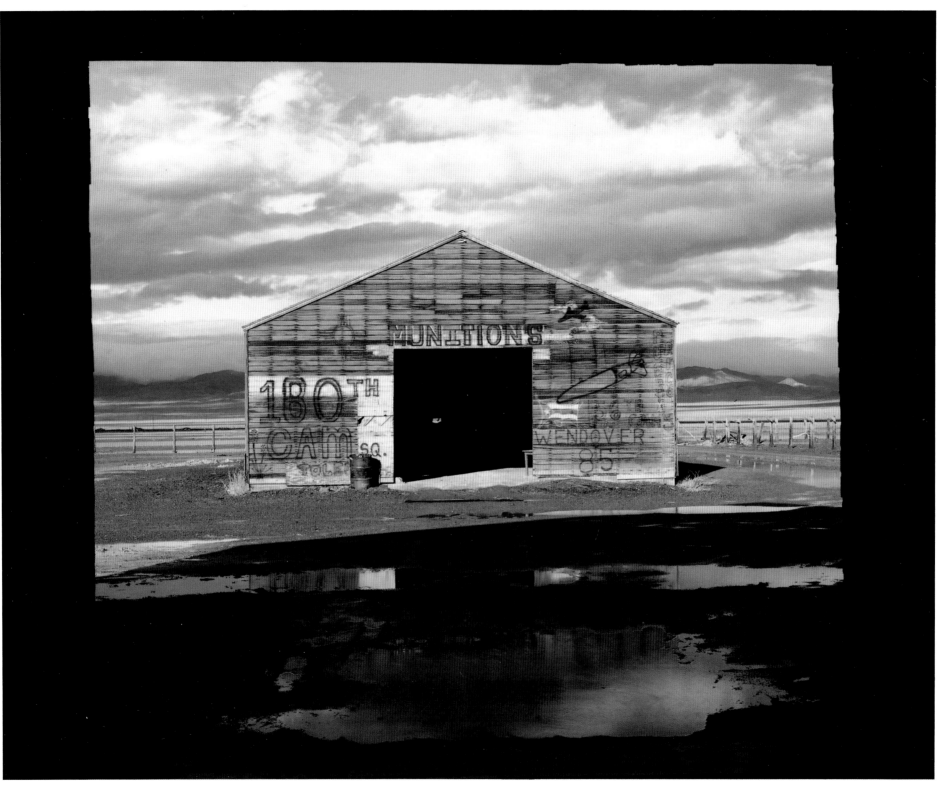

W-47 PROJECT ADMINISTRATION BUILDING

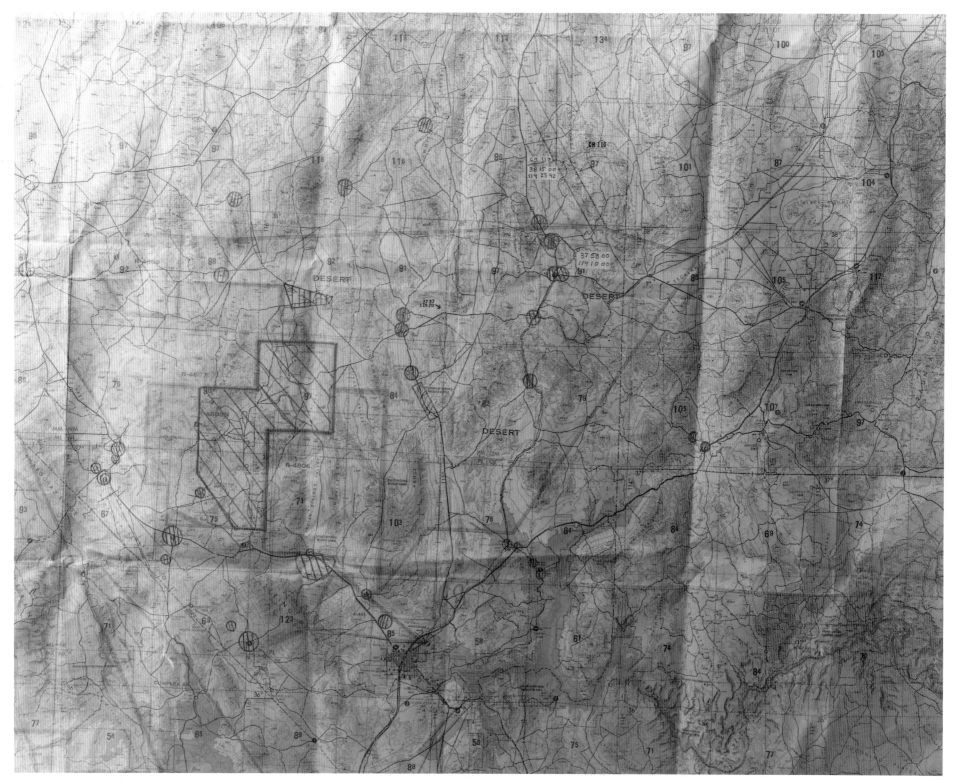

tactical pilotage chart OF THE WESTERN UNITED STATES (large cross-hatched area is the Nuclear Test Site, Nevada), HANGAR OF THE *ENOLA GAY*

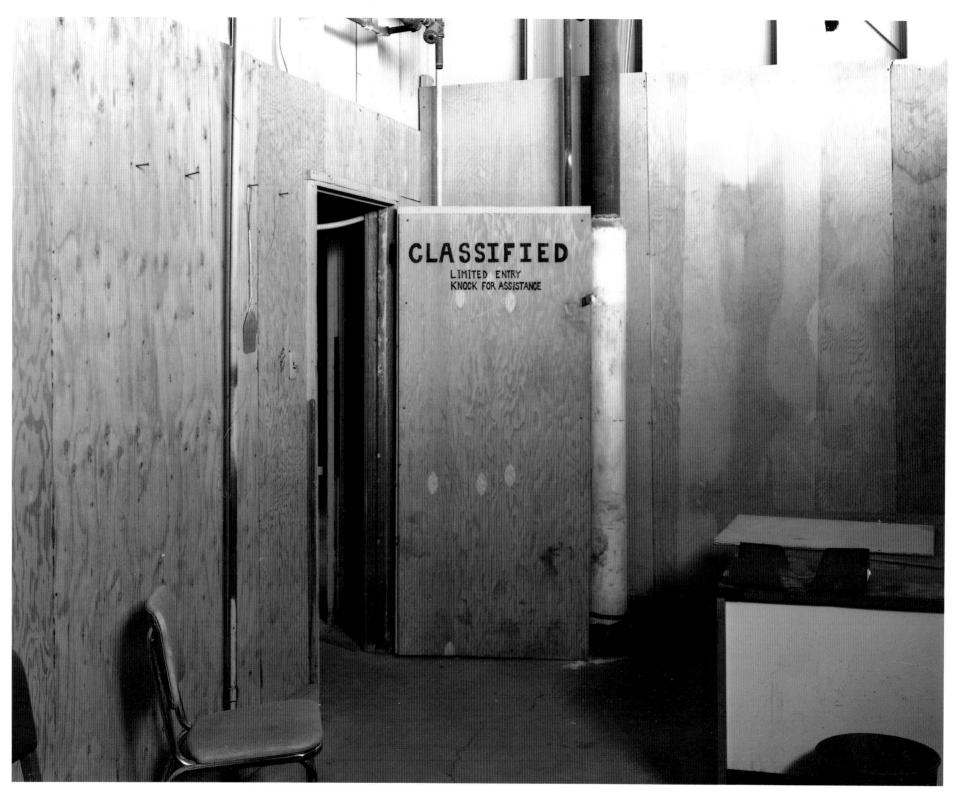

OFFICE, HANGAR OF THE *ENOLA GAY*, 1989

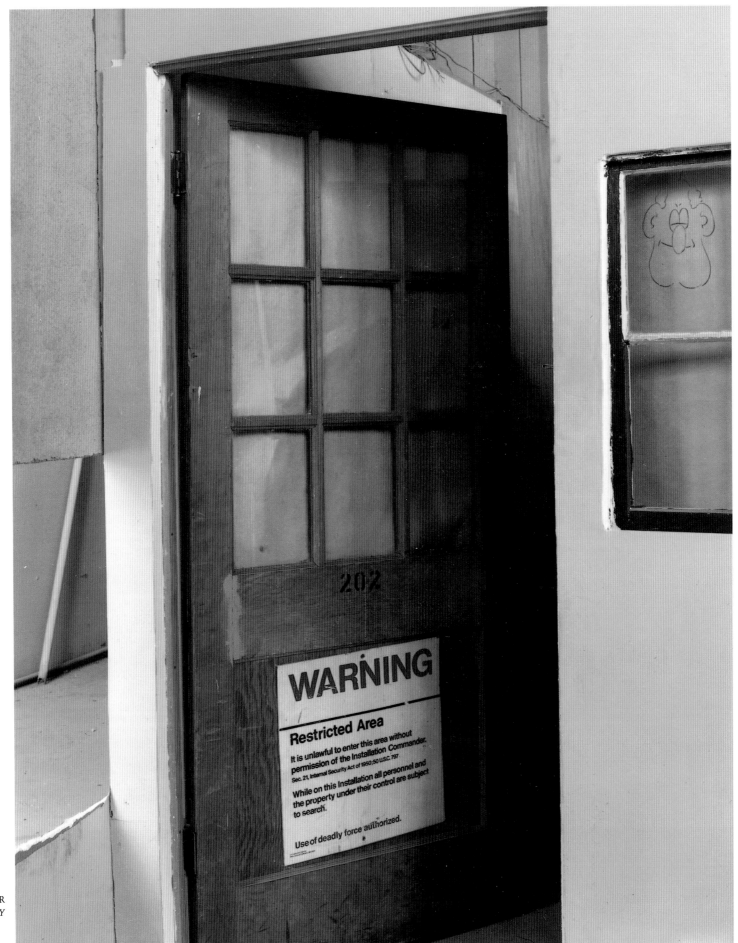

WARNING

Restricted Area

It is unlawful to enter this area without permission of the Installation Commander.
Sec. 21, Internal Security Act of 1950; 50 U.S.C. 797

While on this Installation all personnel and the property under their control are subject to search.

Use of deadly force authorized.

RESTRICTED AREA, HANGAR
OF THE *ENOLA GAY*

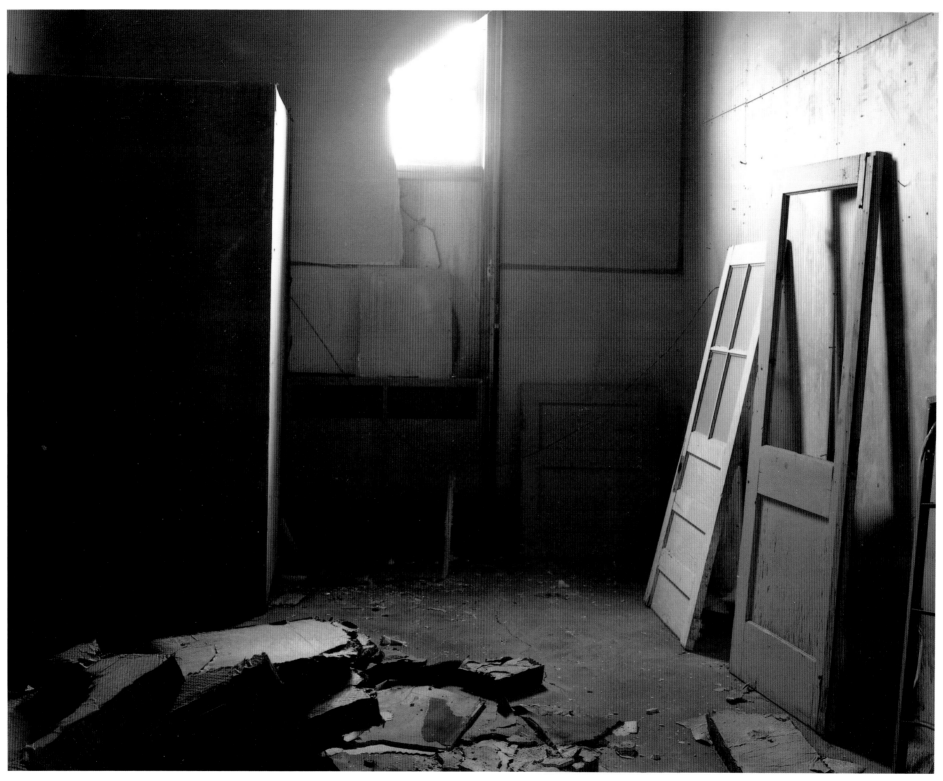

OFFICE, HANGAR OF THE *ENOLA GAY*

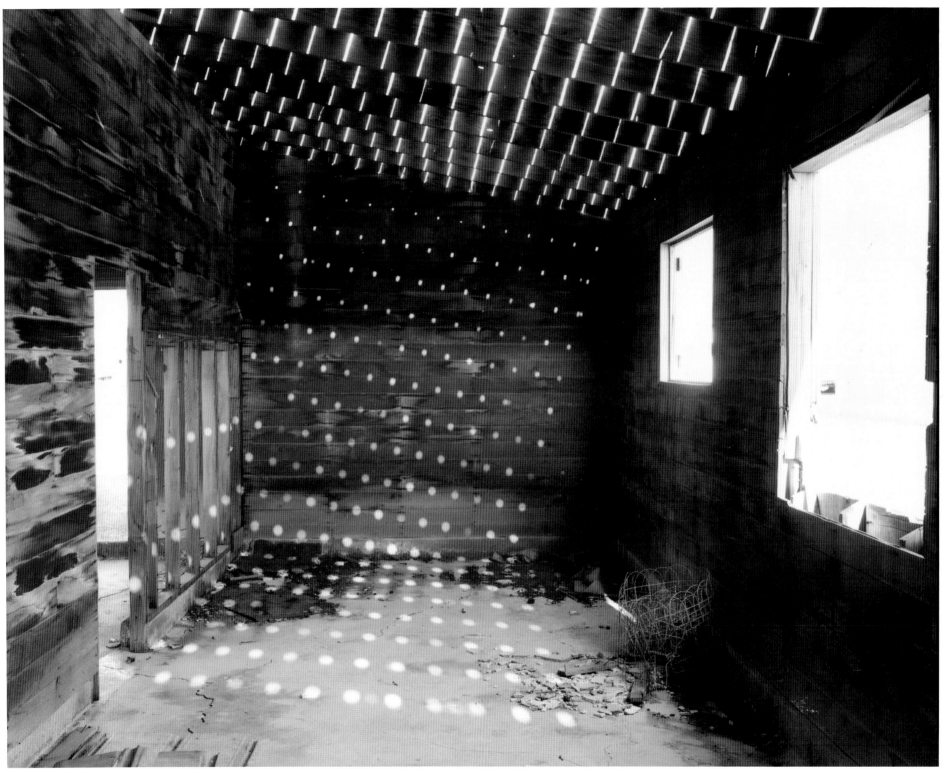

OFFICE, PROJECT SUPPORT HANGAR

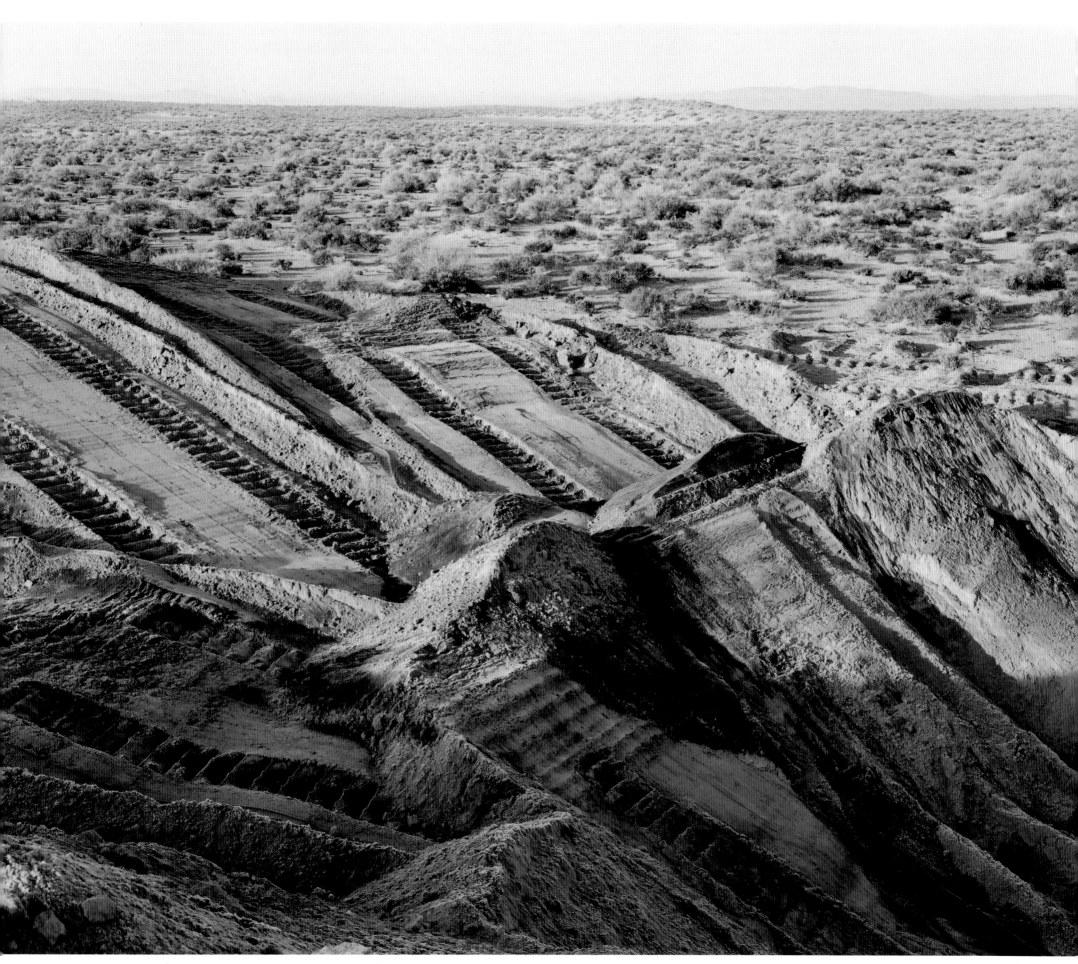

DEAD ANIMALS #268

the pit

On March 24, 1953, the Bulloch brothers were trailing 2,000 head of sheep across the Sand Springs Valley when they were exposed to extensive fallout from a dirty atomic test. Within a week the first ewes began dropping their lambs prematurely—stunted, woolless, legless, potbellied. Soon full-grown sheep started dying in large numbers with running sores, large pustules, and hardened hooves. Horses and cattle were found dead with beta burns. At final count, 4,390 animals were killed.

Initial investigations by government experts indicated that radiation was the cause. However, when the Atomic Energy Commission recognized the potential economic and political liability, all reports and findings were immediately classified. The AEC did provide a public explanation: a dry year and malnutrition were blamed.

Today, county-designated dead-animal pits can be found throughout the West. They function much like trash dumps in which locals are encouraged to deposit livestock that die suddenly. The causes of the animals' deaths are often unknown.

("The Pit" photographs were taken between 1987 and 1989)

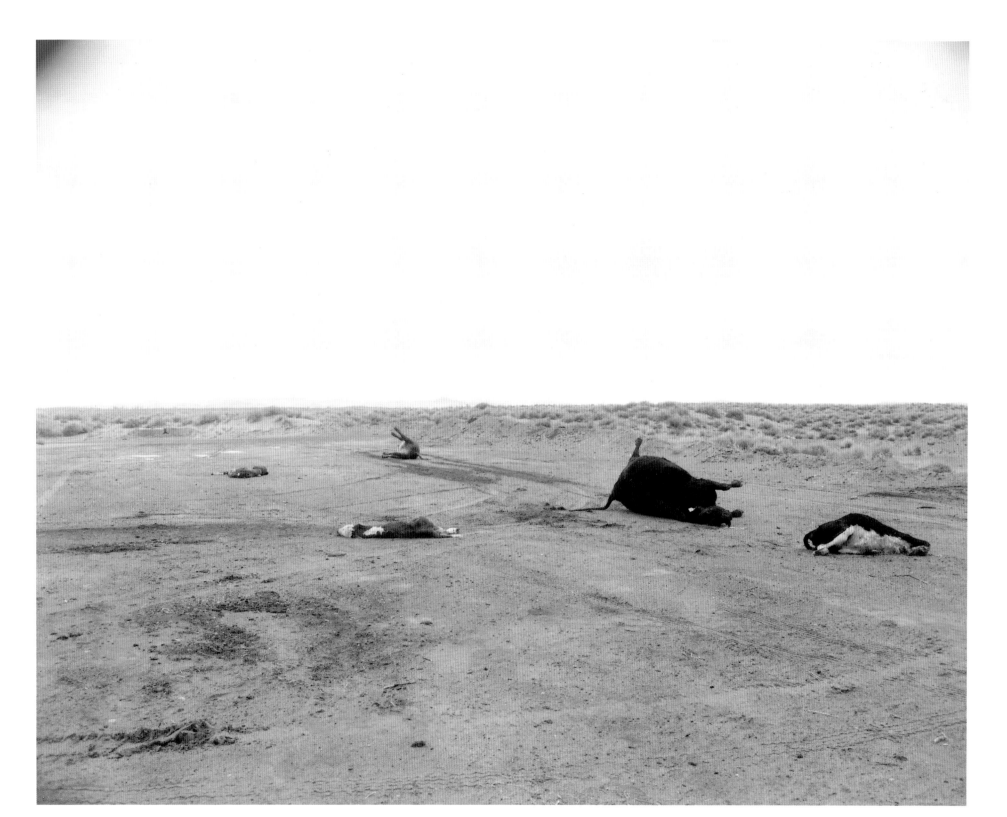

DEAD ANIMALS #112

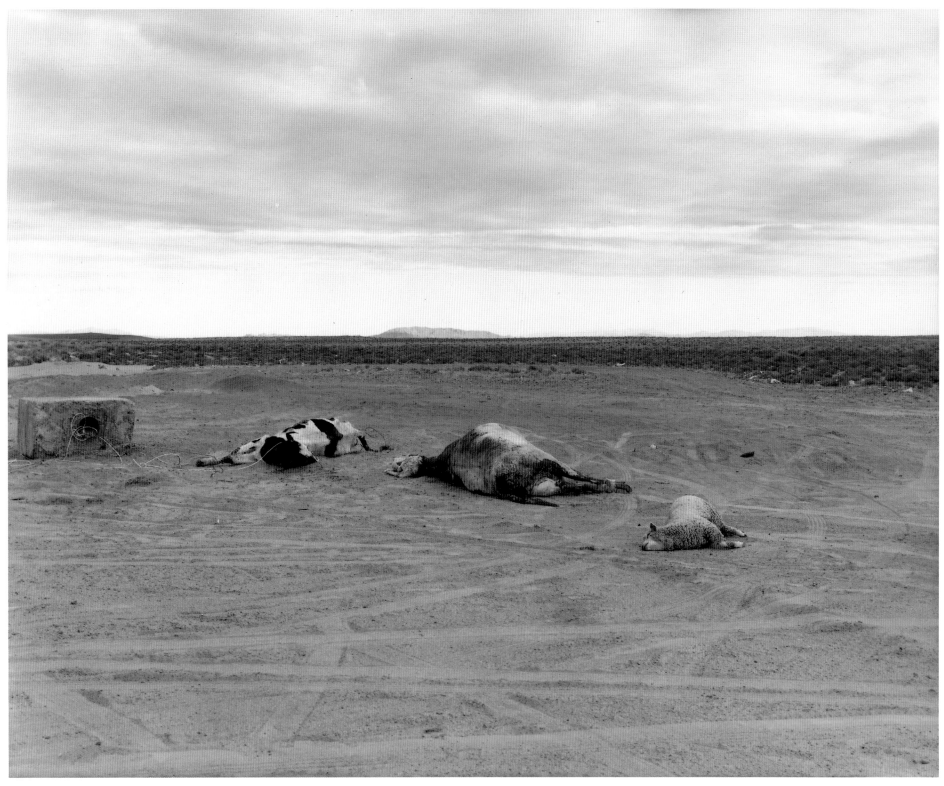

DEAD ANIMALS #324

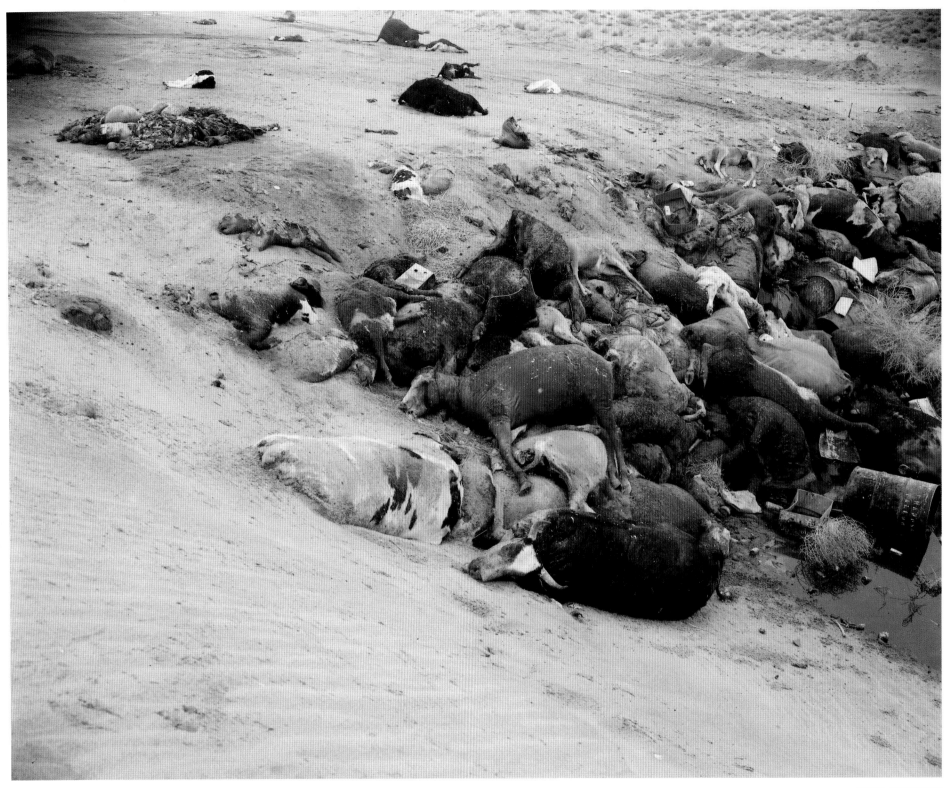

DEAD ANIMALS #1

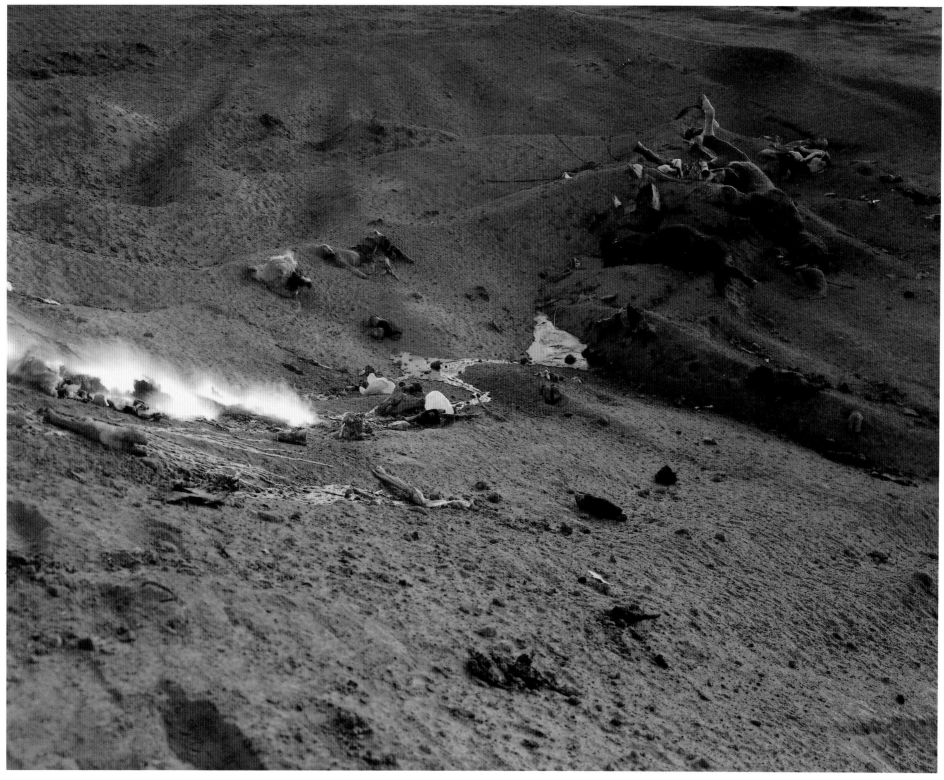

DEAD ANIMALS #362

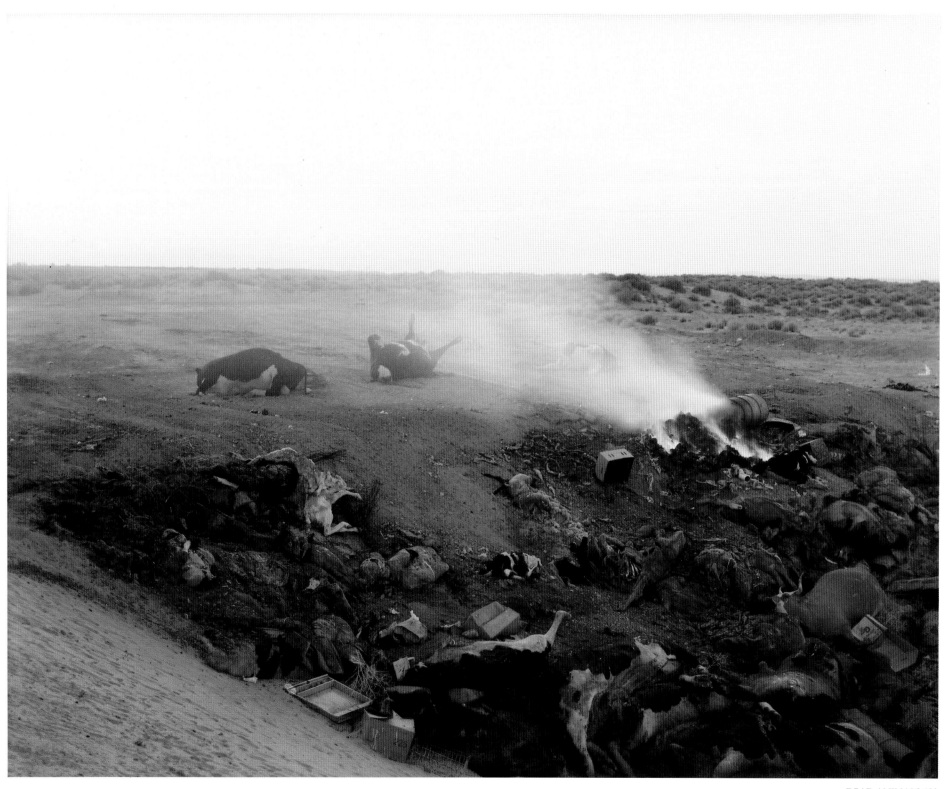

DEAD ANIMALS #93

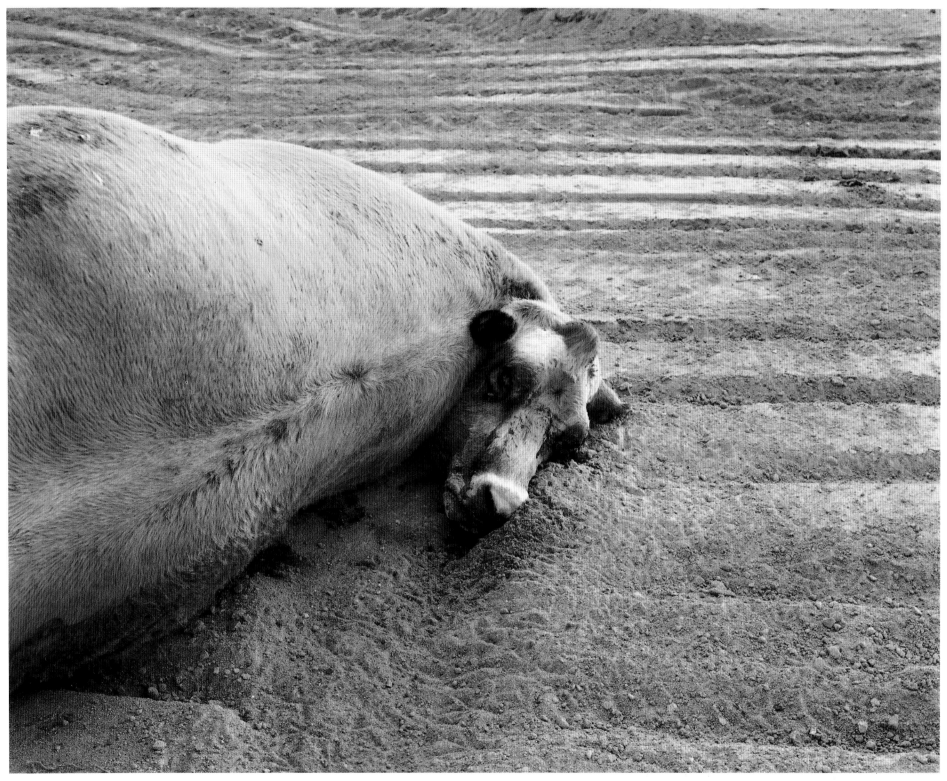

DEAD ANIMALS #454

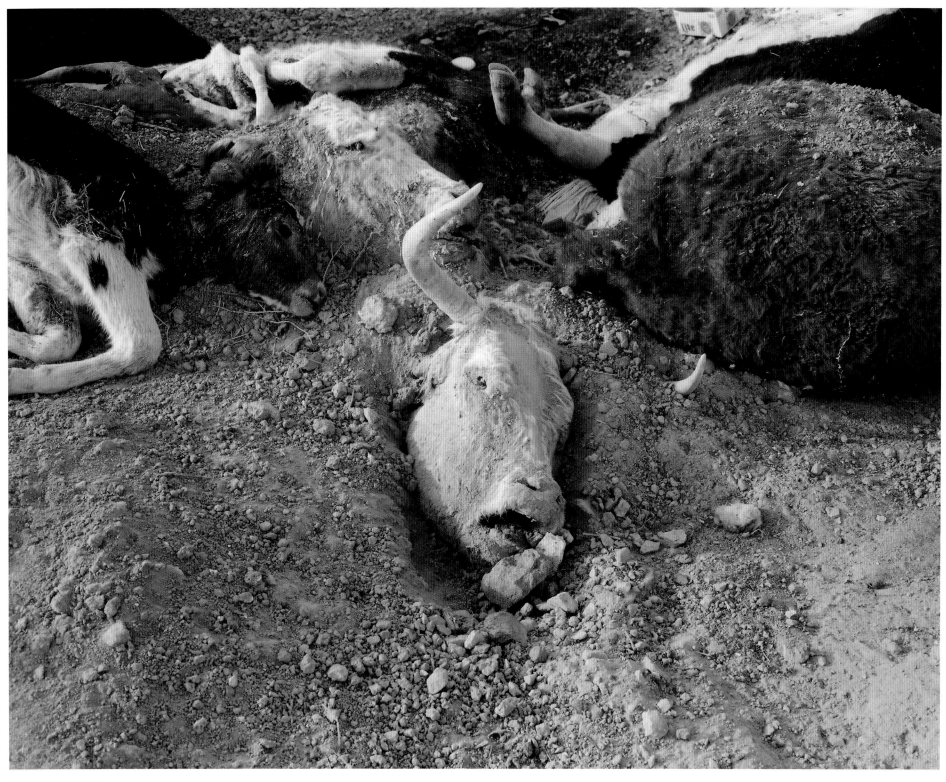

DEAD ANIMALS #86

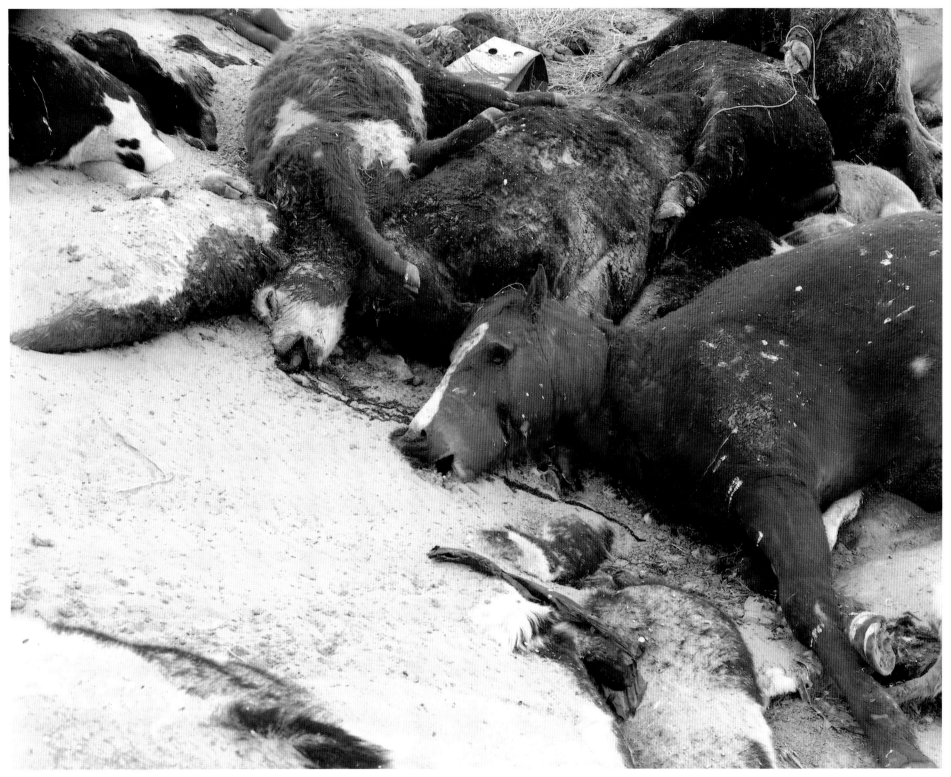

DEAD ANIMALS #20

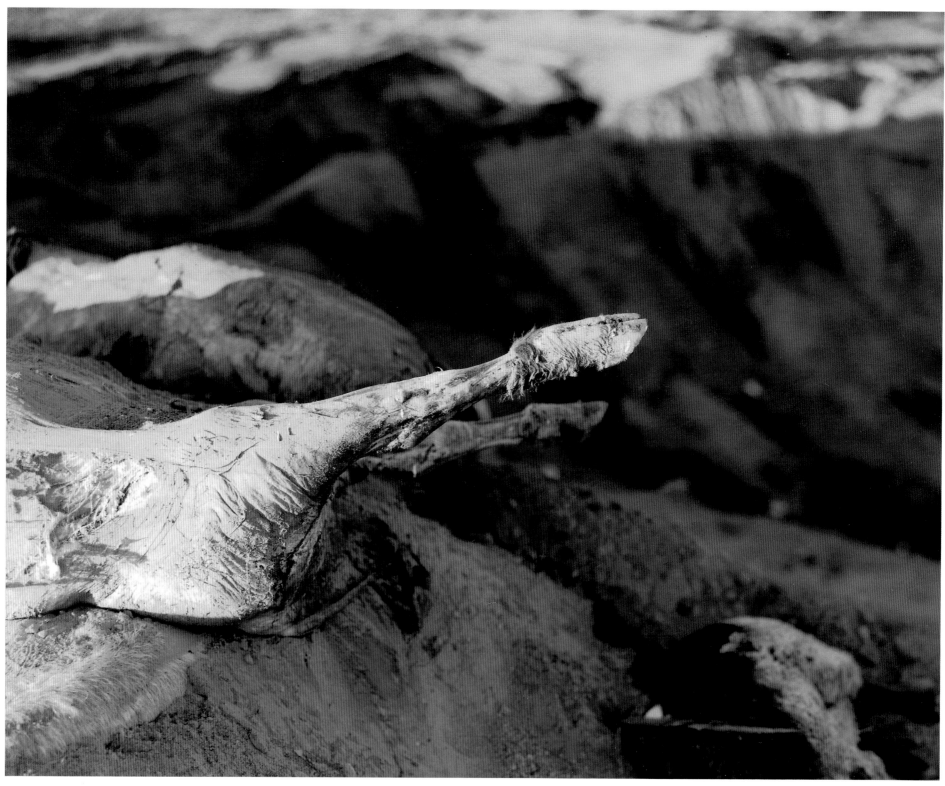

DEAD ANIMALS #363

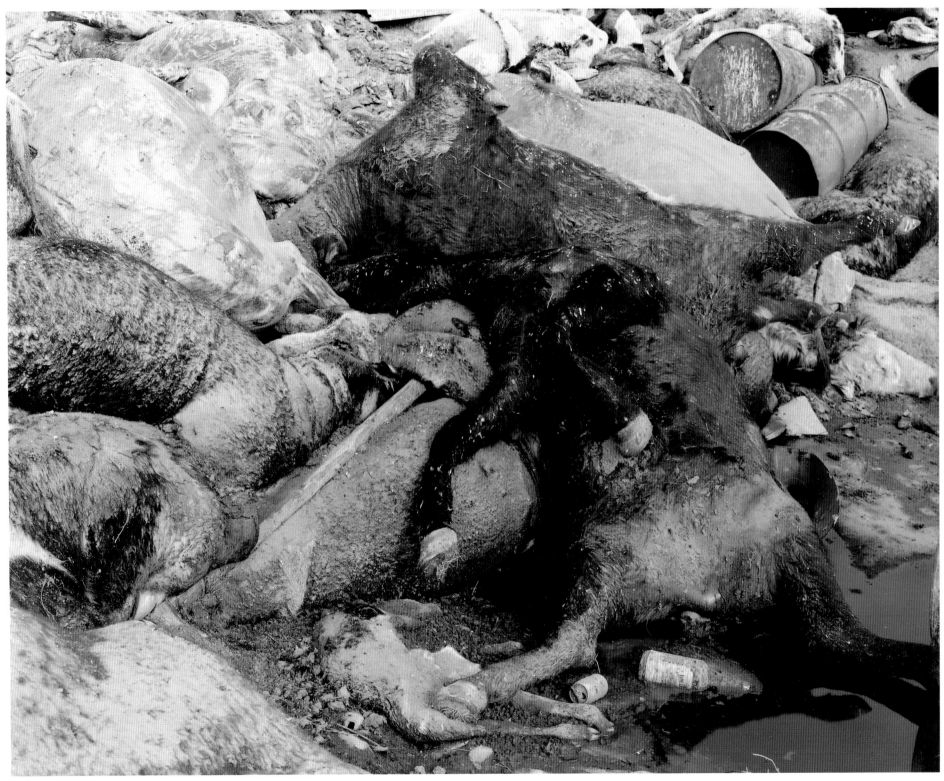

DEAD ANIMALS #147

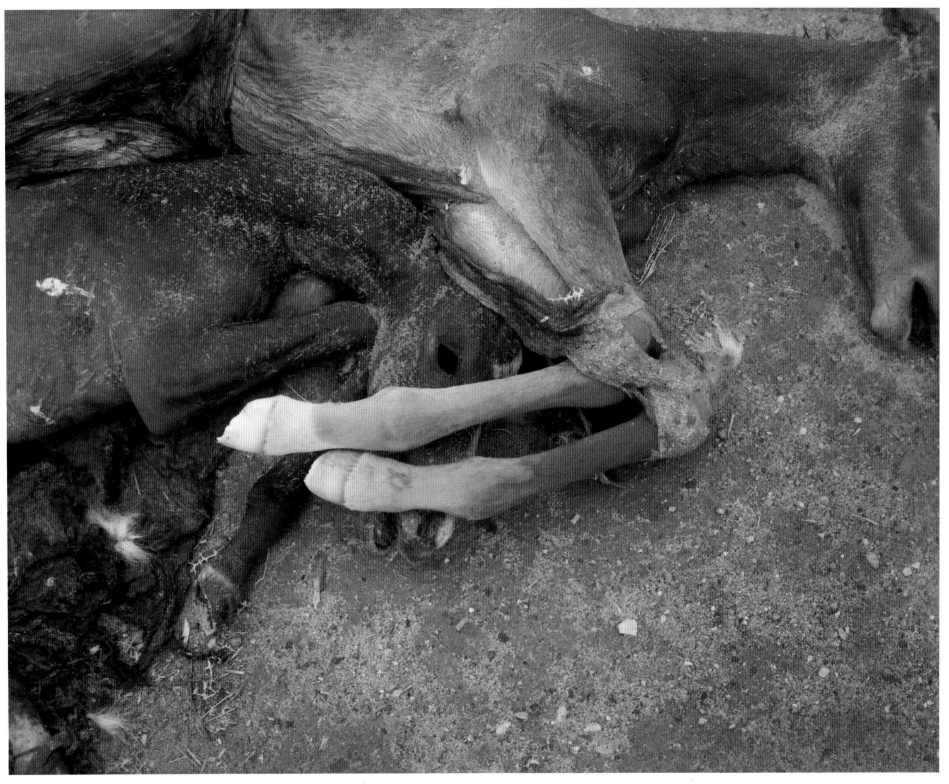

DEAD ANIMALS #79

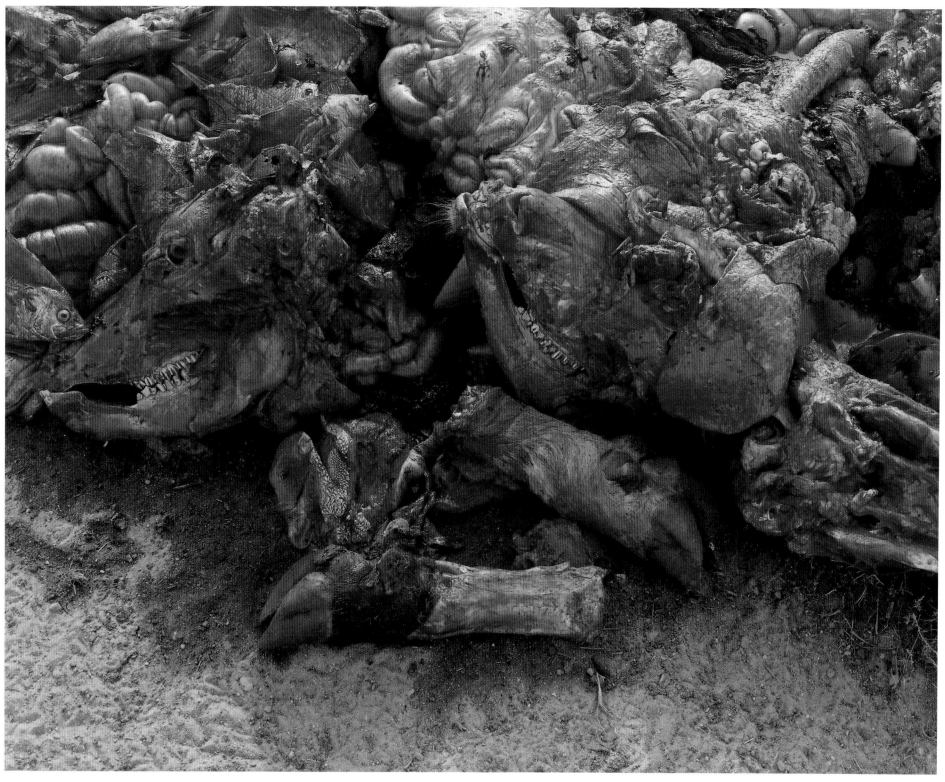

DEAD ANIMALS #78

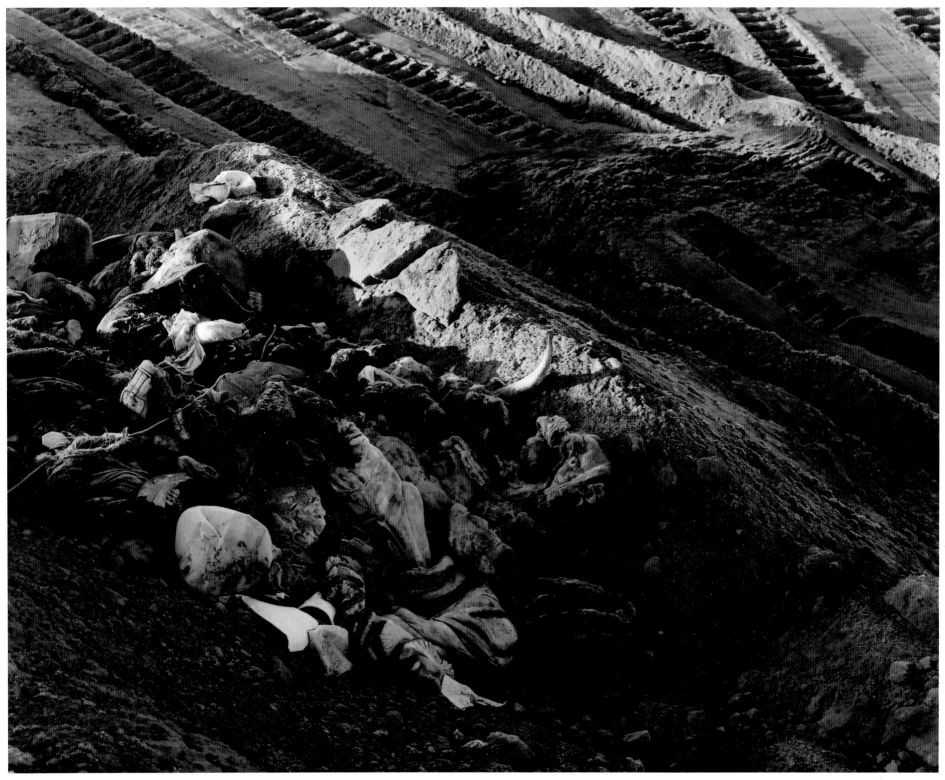

DEAD ANIMALS #293

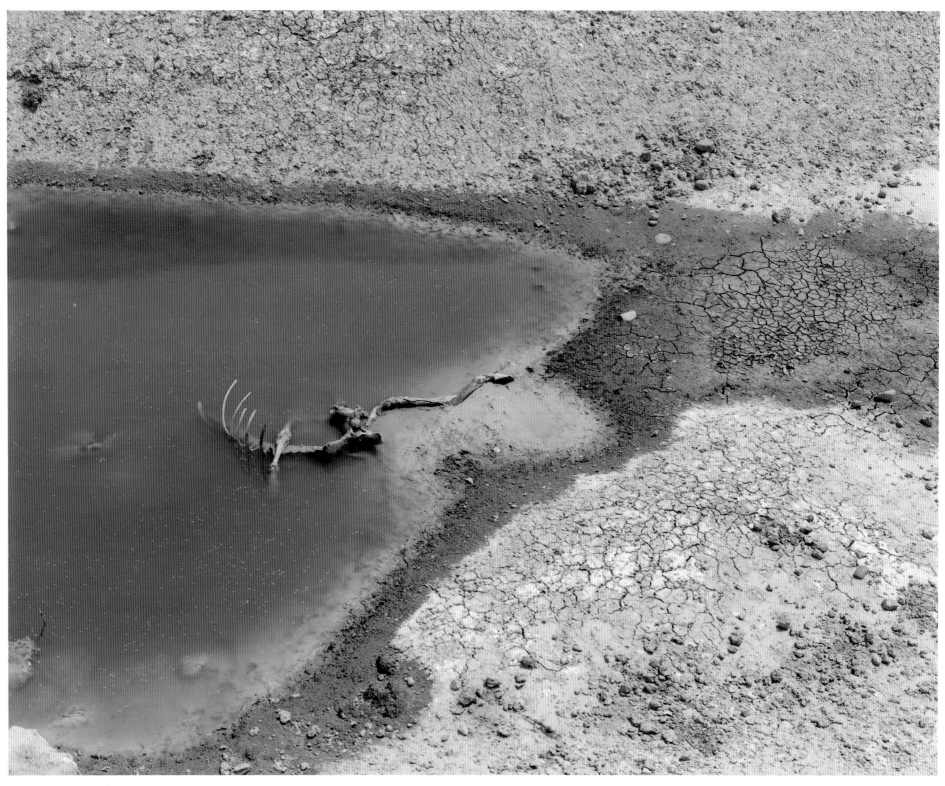

DEAD ANIMALS #77

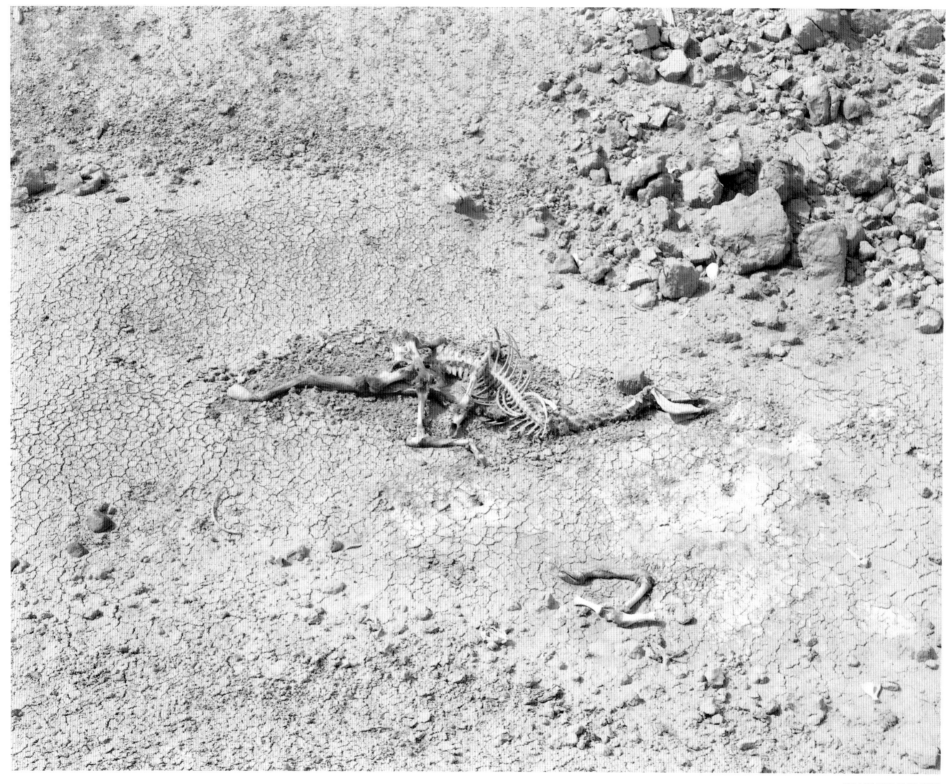

DEAD ANIMALS #137

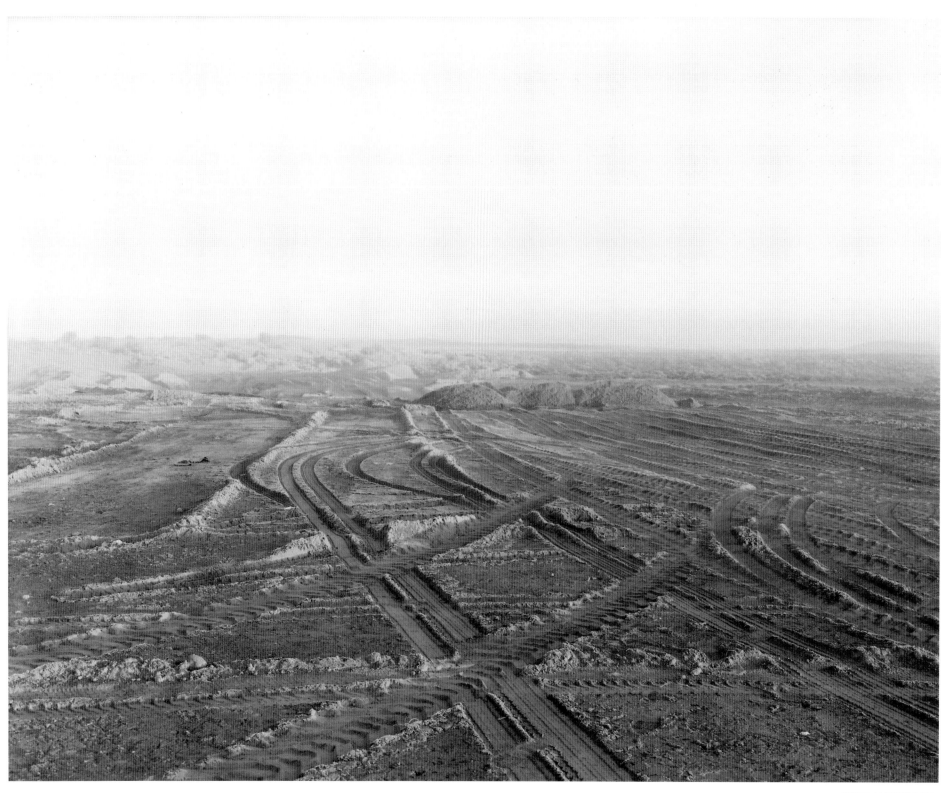

DEAD ANIMALS #294

PLAYBOY

ENTERTAINMENT FOR MEN

VEMBER 1985 • $3.50

THE WOMEN
OF MENSA

AMERICA'S
SMARTEST
FEMALES
POSE NUDE

PLUS: STING
MODERN GIRLS
"MIAMI VICE"
USIC BALLOT

the playboys

Two *Playboy* magazines used for target practice by persons unknown were found at the northwest corner of the Nuclear Test Site in Nevada. Although the women on the covers were the intended targets, all aspects of American culture, as reflected inside the magazines, were riddled with violence.

("The Playboys" were made between 1989 and 1991)

OPPOSITE: COVER, NOVEMBER 1985 ISSUE OF *PLAYBOY* MAGAZINE, 1989

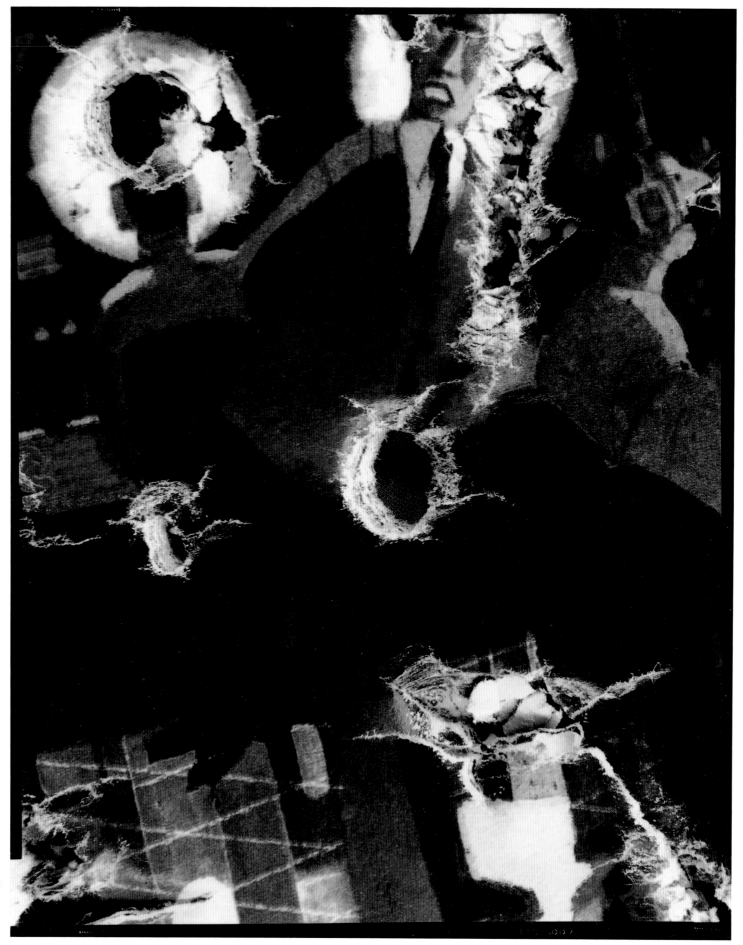

PLAYBOY #96 (CASTRATO)

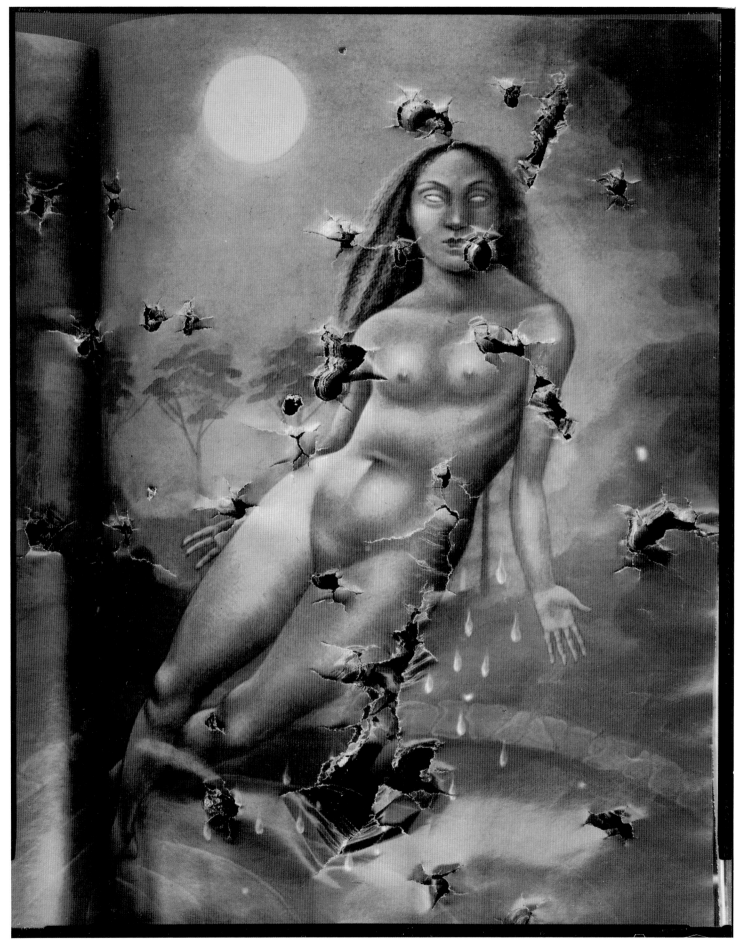

PLAYBOY #5 (MULATTA)

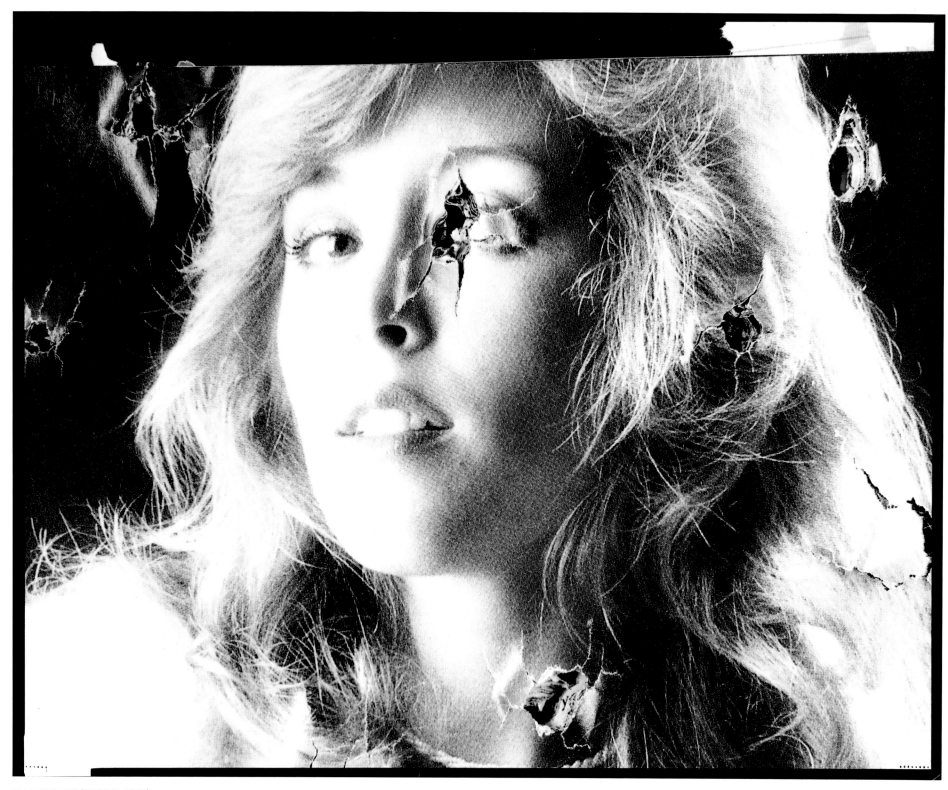

PLAYBOY #172 (DONNA RICE)

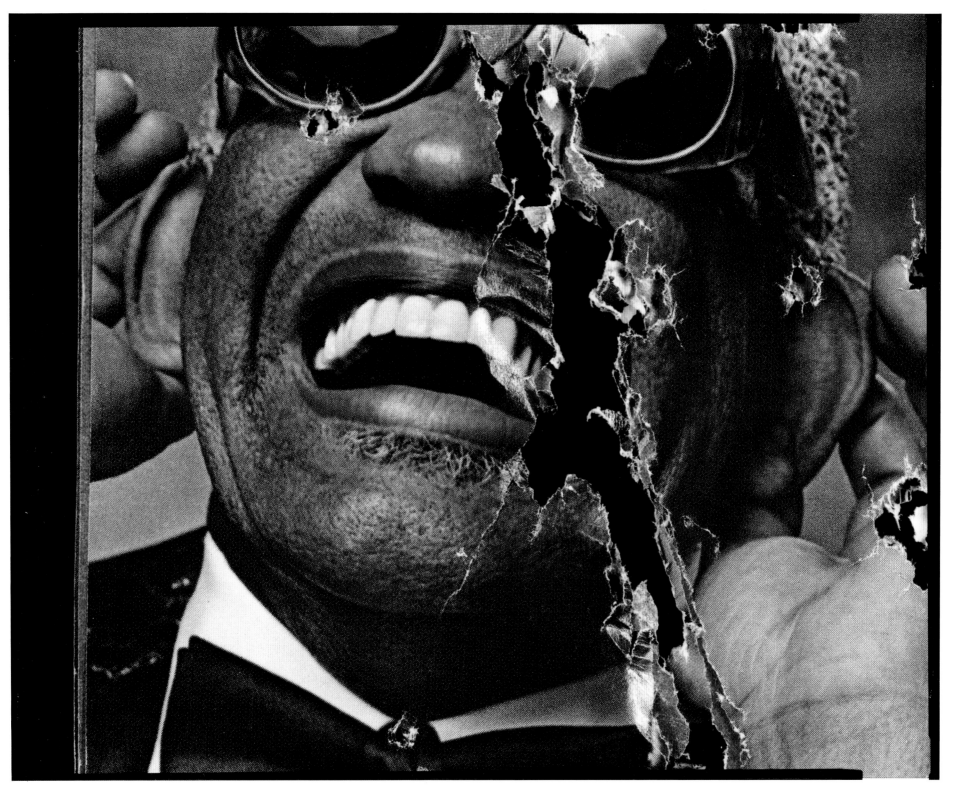

PLAYBOY #94 (RAY CHARLES)

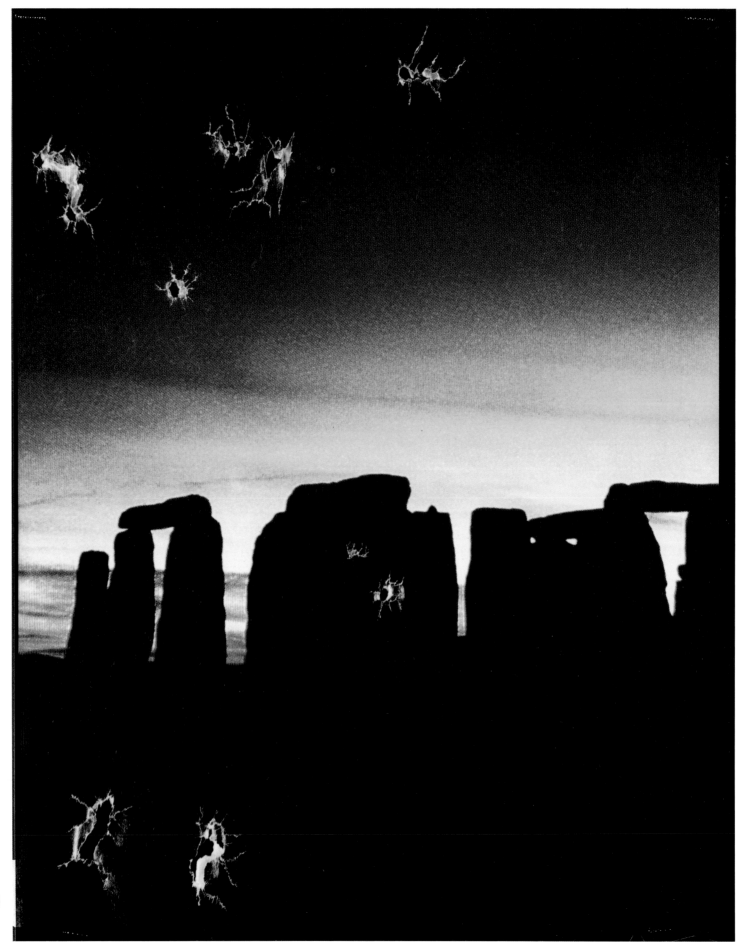

PLAYBOY #143 (STONEHENGE)

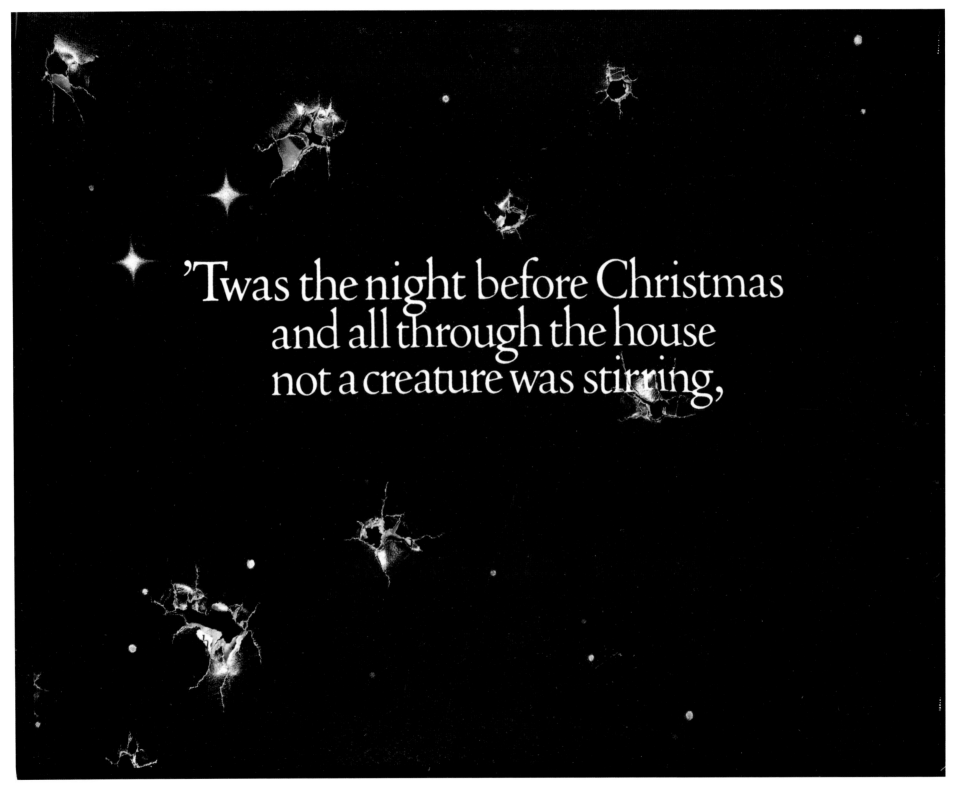

'Twas the night before Christmas
and all through the house
not a creature was stirring,

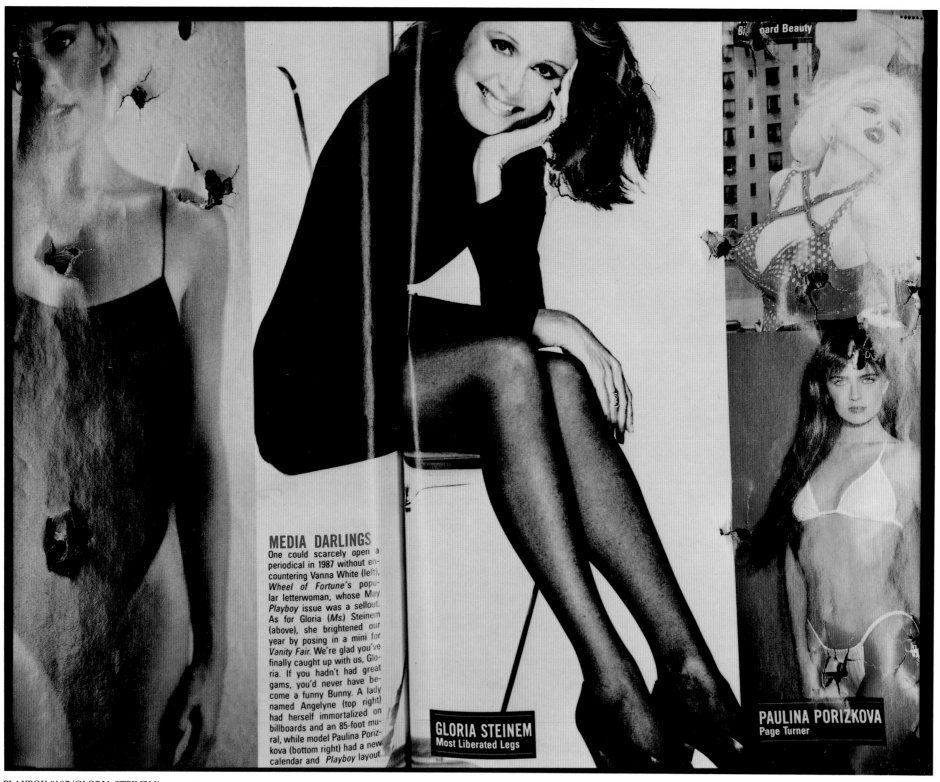

MEDIA DARLINGS

One could scarcely open a periodical in 1987 without encountering Vanna White (left), *Wheel of Fortune*'s popular letterwoman, whose May *Playboy* issue was a sellout. As for Gloria (*Ms.*) Steinem (above), she brightened our year by posing in a mini for *Vanity Fair*. We're glad you've finally caught up with us, Gloria. If you hadn't had great gams, you'd never have become a funny Bunny. A lady named Angelyne (top right) had herself immortalized on billboards and an 85-foot mural, while model Paulina Porizkova (bottom right) had a new calendar and *Playboy* layout.

GLORIA STEINEM
Most Liberated Legs

PAULINA PORIZKOVA
Page Turner

PLAYBOY #187 (GLORIA STEINEM)

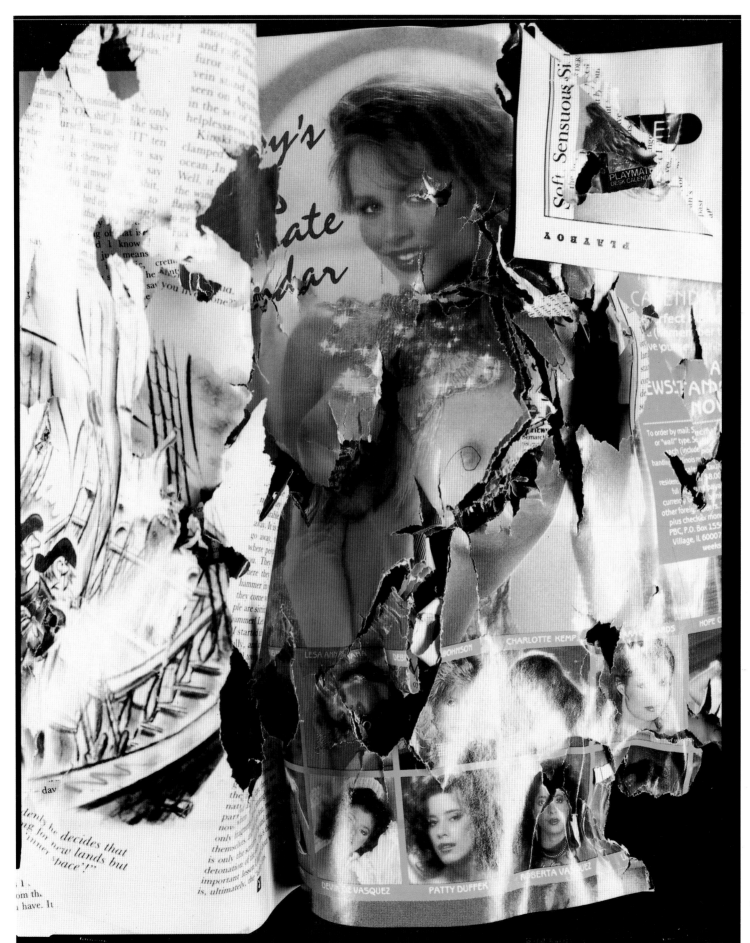

PLAYBOY #80
(PLAYMATE CALENDAR)

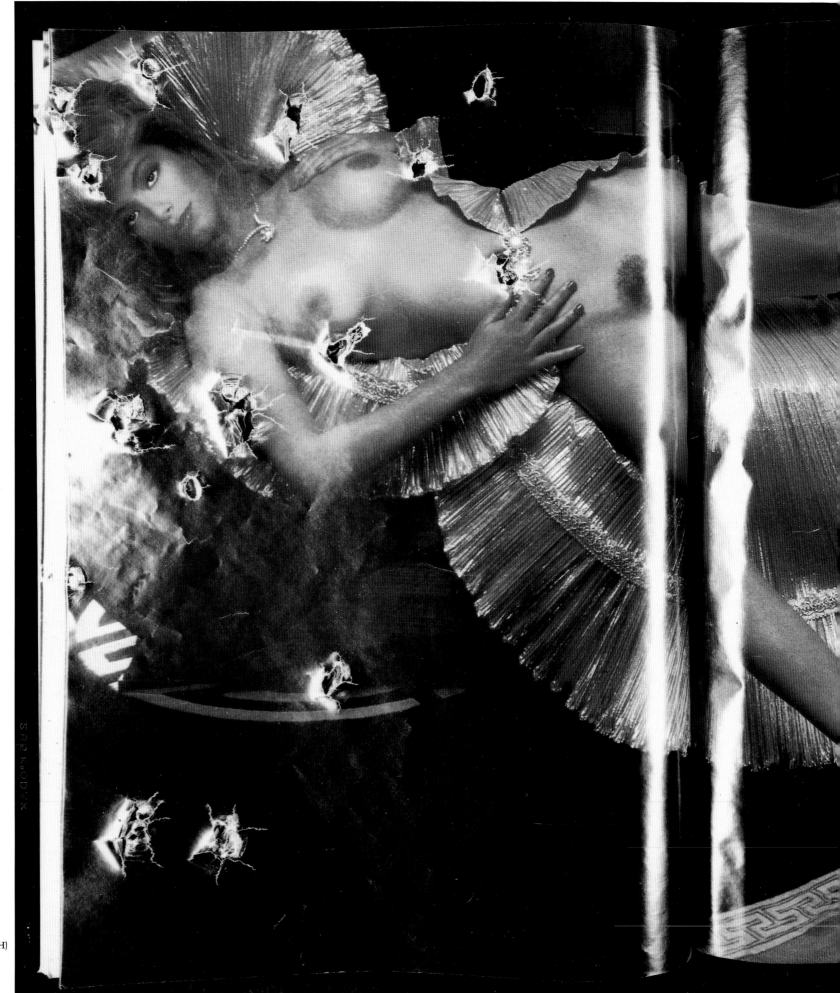

PLAYBOY #39 (PLAYMATE OF THE MONTH)

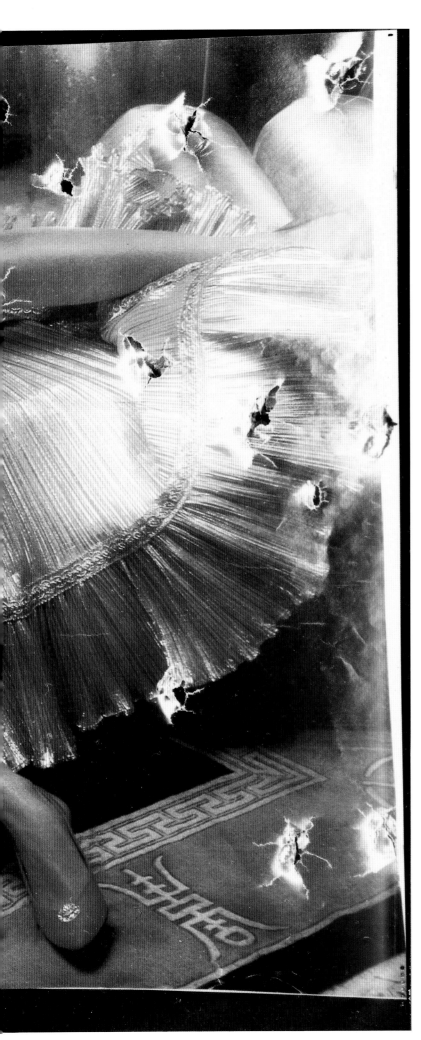

very difficult scientific ideas. He introduced me to Jung's, and I would never have read Jung if I had read Koestler. He has been criticized for being a jack-of-all-trades and a master of none, but God, we need people like that, because the scientific community and the lay community have never been so far apart. We have people making executive decisions at a government level who don't even know the second law of thermodynamics. Who does? So, anyway, those explorations were personal revelations to me, and they also have given me so much more to draw on.

PLAYBOY: How have these revelations affected your life?

STING: The most significant effect was realization that I can use the demonic side me to create. I don't have to suffer and be miserable to create. I thought I did. I thought the only way to operate was by creating conflict, tension, putting pressure on myself and other people. But now I think differently. I think there's a way of inspiring yourself from inside in positive way. It's a very negative thing to have to live through crisis in order to write and perform. It's self-destructive and a bit of a cliché. Once you get inside it, there's no way out except madness, and I really don't want to become mad. I'm very much afraid of being mad—that's my one fear.

PLAYBOY: Are you a candidate?

STING: For madness? Um, I have been. As an artist, you are sort of forced to look into that side of yourself by the nature of what you do, and if you look too closely, you tend to be drawn into it—the dark side of you, really, the shadow, in Jungian terms. You have to be able to control the thing and get to know it and not be overwhelmed by it. Your shadow is very creative. It's when you are most in touch with your feelings and emotions, your essence.

PLAYBOY: Would you go so far as to sabotage a relationship to stir things up?

STING: I think I've been in great danger of doing that, both in my personal relationships and in my relationships with the people I make music with. I seem to thrive on friction, or I have in the past, and I have deliberately set out to cause friction. I am sure there are other more gentle and, I hope, more profound ways of doing it.

PLAYBOY: Such as?

STING: There's no one thing. I've grown. I consider myself an adult now. I write and perform as an adult—not as a petulant schoolboy, though I can still lapse into that sort of mind-set. I've also started to use my dream life much more than I ever did. Last night I never dreamed. People would say, "What did you dream last night?" I'd tell them I never had a dream in my life. It was only when I

PLAYBOY: For example?

STING: I was in my back garden. It's a small, narrow garden, with walls and ivy all around it, and there are flower beds, beautifully cut lawns and little zigzag pathways, plants, roses—really rather nice. And I'm, in one of the walls, this big hole appeared, and out of it crawled these four enormous, prehistoric blue turtles with these wonderful scaly necks and fantastic heads. They were kind of drunk on their own virility, very athletic and *macho,* and they were showing off in my back garden, doing back flips, jumping on tables and smashing glasses. And in the process of this athletic, drunken display, they completely destroyed my beautiful garden. In the dream, I wasn't pissed at this. I was even enjoying the fact that the garden was being wrecked. I was sort of into it. It was such a wonderful spectacle.

Well, it was this dream that made me realize that I had to do this record—I had to stir things up. The garden was my safe life in The Police. The turtles were Kenny, Omar, Branford and all the musicians I am working with. That's why the album is *The Dream of the Blue Turtles.* The fact that the turtles destroyed the garden was to me a confirmation that I was on the right track—what I was doing was the right thing for me. And I wrote this wacky piece of music to go with it, this weird ersatz jazz. It makes sense after you've heard the dream.

PLAYBOY: How has this self-discovery affected your personal life?

STING: I am far more secure. I don't have to rely on the people around me. I don't have close-knit coterie of friends, I have about three, very close friends who know me very well, but apart from that, there is a huge variety of people I like, and I have friendly relations with, I think it is wrong and very unwise to limit your sociability to what you feel safe with, or people you pay. I have friends who are as esteemed and powerful in their own worlds as I am in mine, and I enjoy their company more than anything else.

PLAYBOY: Are you all of this serious?

STING: Me? No, I'm a complete maniac. I really have my moments of madness, though few people are privy to them. It takes one of the people close to me to bring me out of myself. I've been known to roll on the floor for half an hour. We were out in the studio sometimes, like the song *The Dream of the Blue Turtles,* which started with me rolling around for 20 minutes—completely and utterly mad, cackling, for no apparent reason. It's a side I show to only a few friends.

PLAYBOY: We ask not just because of this

and think I'm always a bit down. I'm not that way at all. I'm fun-loving. I like messing around, but it has never stopped me from switching over. I really don't know whether I would choose the Van Gogh or the Paul McCartney school of art. Is there anything in between? [*Laughs*]

All in all, I've emerged, I think, in pretty good shape. I didn't take the other ways out—drugs, which are always there as a crutch, always around you, especially in rock 'n' roll. The rock-'n'-roll cliché: "Hope I die before I get old. Live and die young, have a beautiful corpse." I've been through all that. I almost did leave a beautiful corpse.

PLAYBOY: Was that period—the break-up of your marriage, your drug use, topped with success?

STING: Yeah, you have all that power and those riches, and your very self just collapses inside. It's not worth a penny. "What's the point of this?" you ask yourself. "Why in the hell am I using all this energy and ultimately achieving this nothingness?" Very serious crisis. Why should I be rewarded with all this money and attention and everything that goes with it? It's weird for me, though I work bloody hard for my money. The attention is hard to take. Suddenly, you have a hit record and a huge following, and if you are a responsible person and you are asked responsible questions, you have to attempt to be coherent about them. If you ask me about nuclear power, I'm supposed to have a responsible answer. I don't know if I'm qualified to have a reasonable answer on every issue, yet I can't just say, "No, no, I don't know anything about it." I have to say what I believe.

Before I was famous, I could vanish; it was quite easy. Now it is much more difficult. It can be a nightmare. I can vanish, because I have money. Even so, I sometimes wake up at night in a cold sweat. I'm objective about who I am, what I am, what I've done, but sometimes you look at yourself and say, "I'm this; I've done this" and people know me as this." Fame means the image is virtually forever. "Didn't you used to be so-and-so? Didn't you used to be that?" People will never treat me as someone with no past. I think that in rock 'n' roll, the blueprint for disaster is clear one. That book has already been written—Elvis Presley, Sid Vicious, Jimi Hendrix. The blueprint for survival hasn't yet been written, in my opinion, and that's a much more original route. I'd like to write it; that's the one I really want to write.

PLAYBOY: Will you write it?

STING: Yes, and it will be just like my songs. The issues may be very serious and

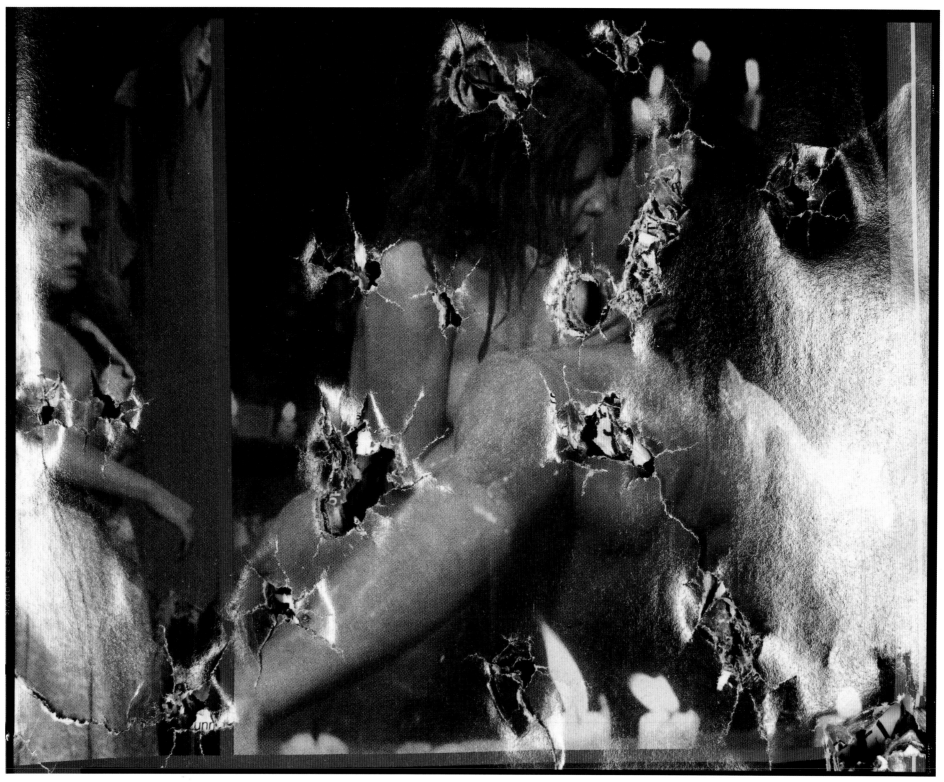

PLAYBOY #23 (THE KISS)

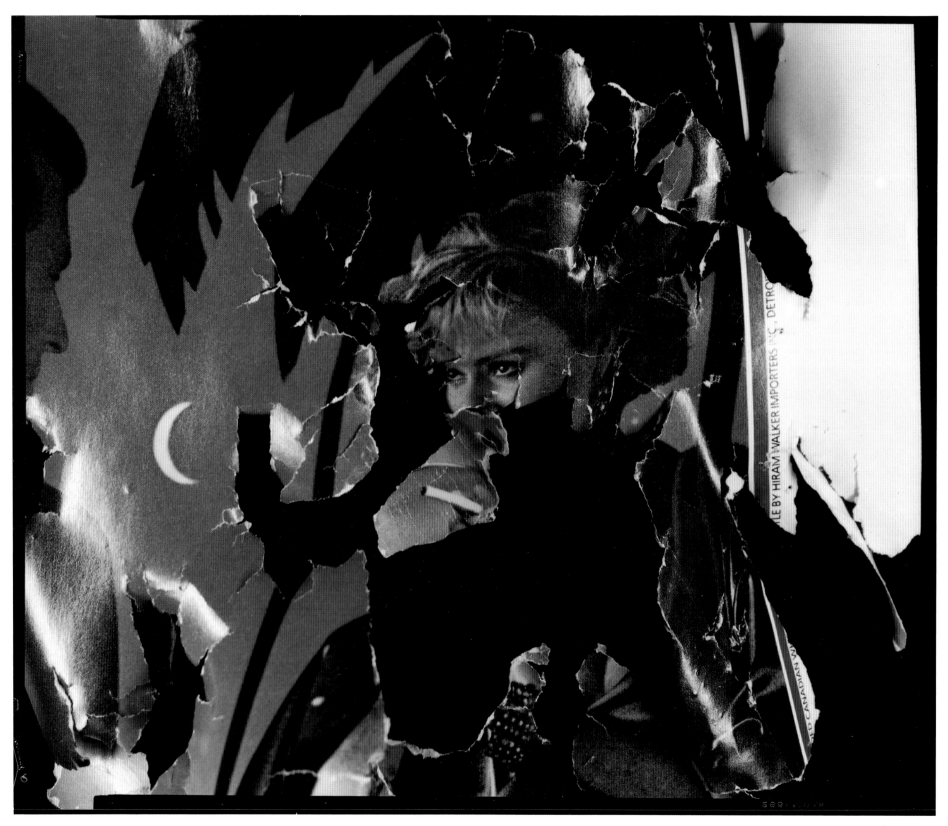

PLAYBOY #41 (THE GAZE)

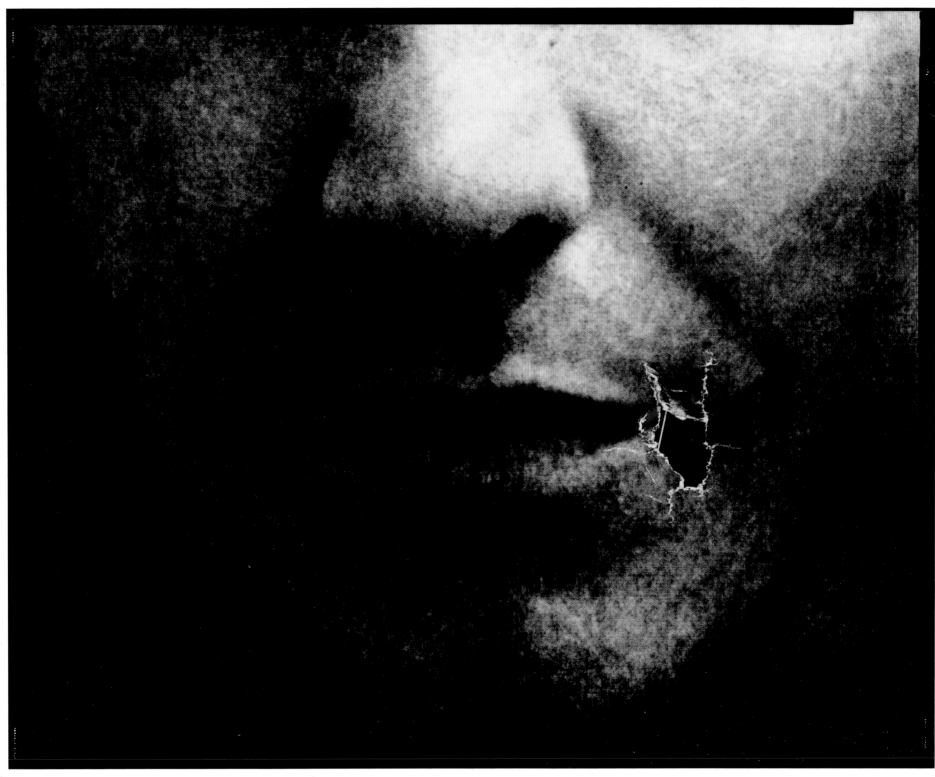

PLAYBOY #157 (DENNIS QUAID)

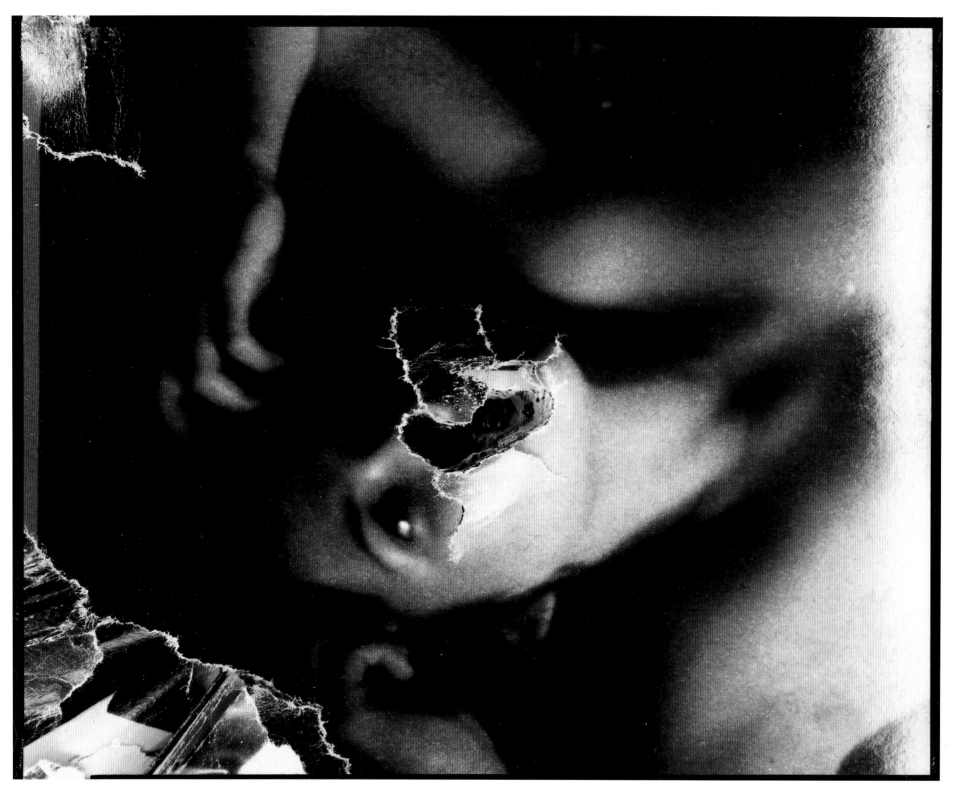

PLAYBOY #90 (HOLE IN THE MOUTH)

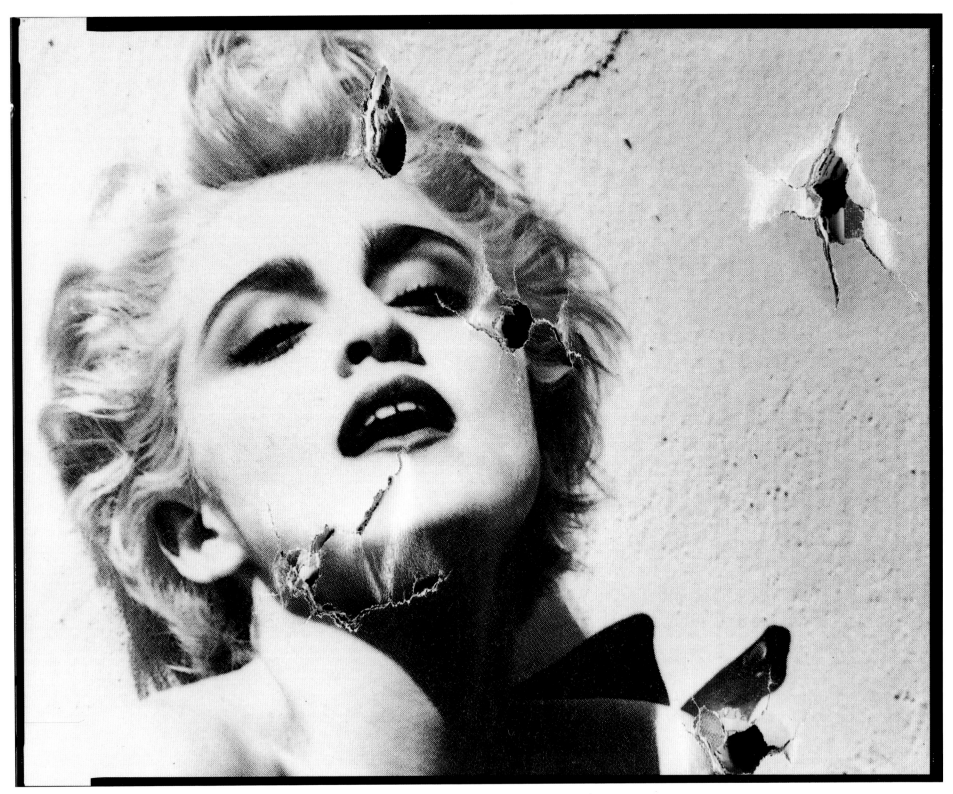

PLAYBOY #92 (MADONNA)

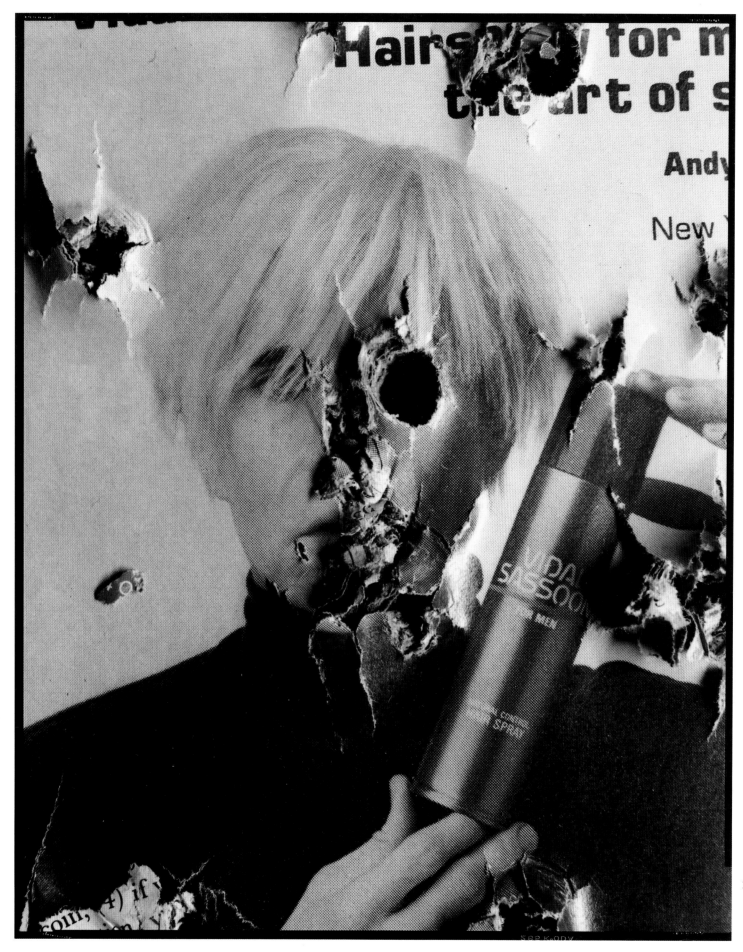

PLAYBOY #38 (WARHOL)

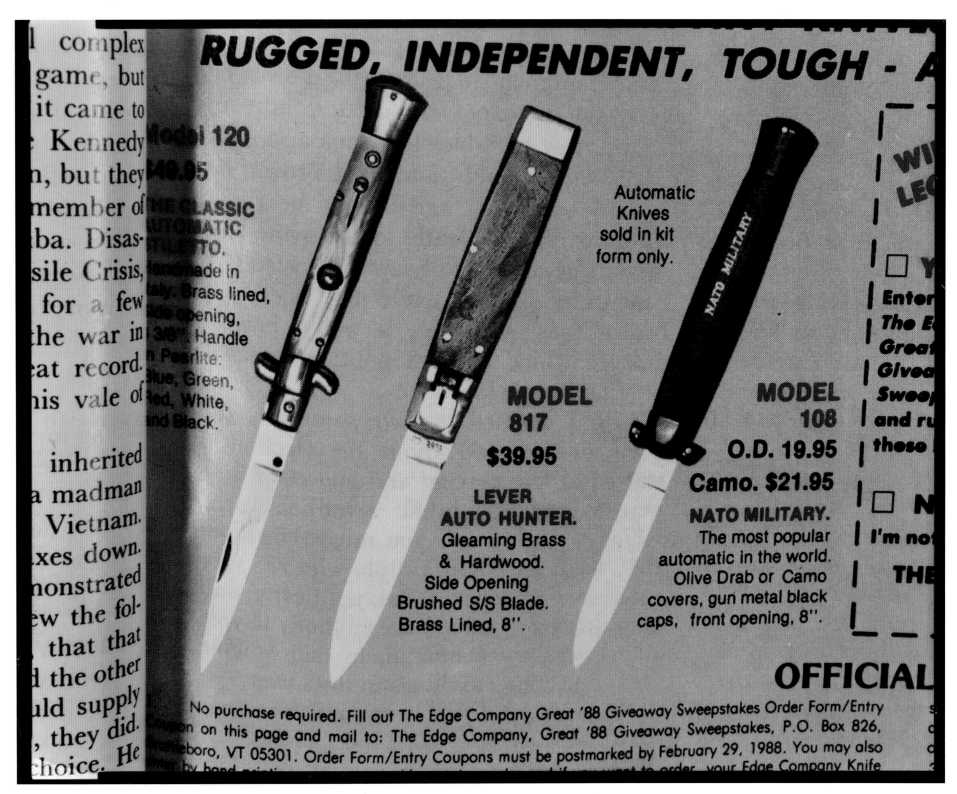

complex
game, but
it came to
Kennedy
, but they
member of
ba. Disas-
sile Crisis,
for a few
the war in
at record.
his vale of

inherited
a madman
Vietnam.
xes down.
onstrated
ew the fol-
that that
the other
uld supply
they did.
choice. He

PLAYBOY #126 (THREE KNIVES)

Sexiest Shredder

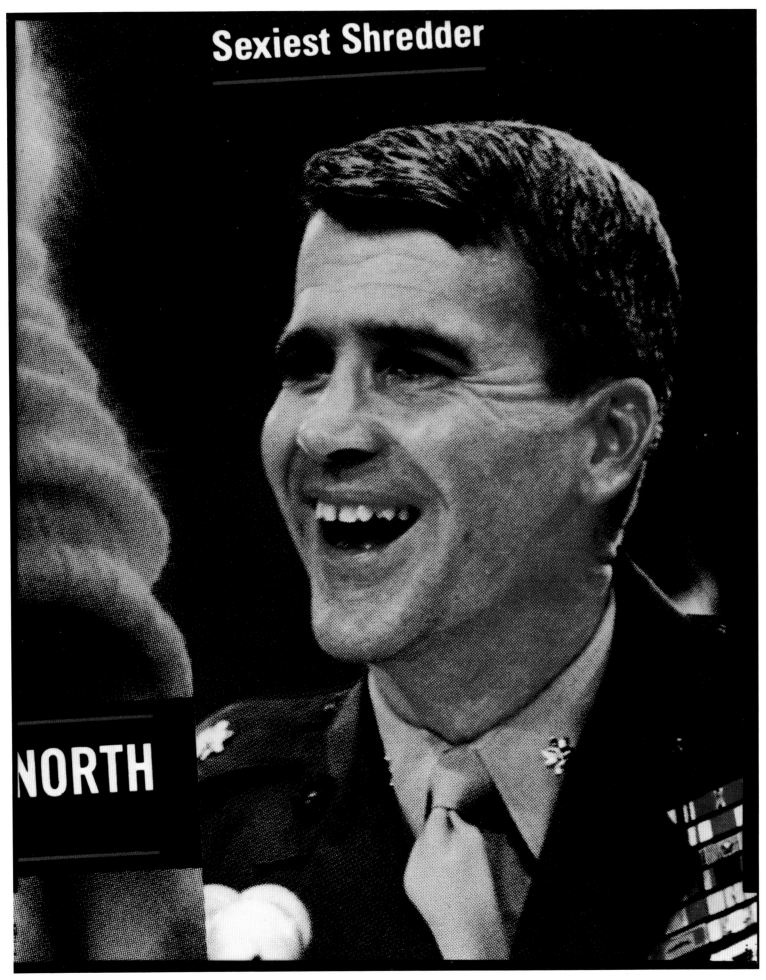

NORTH

PLAYBOY #182 (OLLIE NORTH)

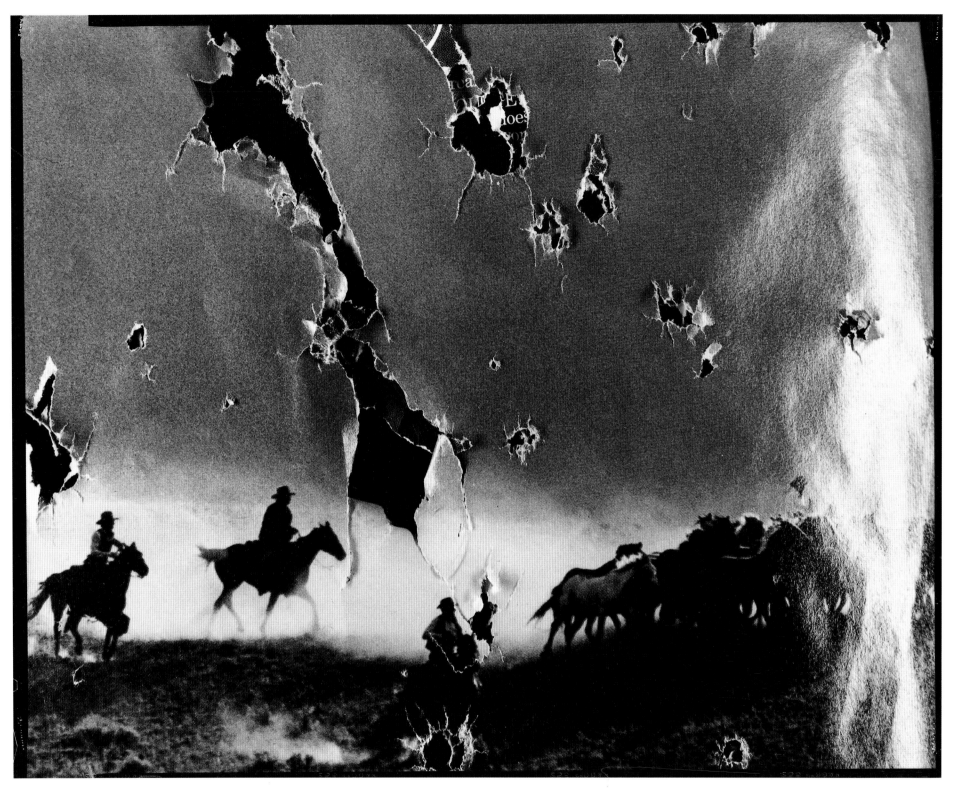

PLAYBOY #97 (MARLBORO COUNTRY)

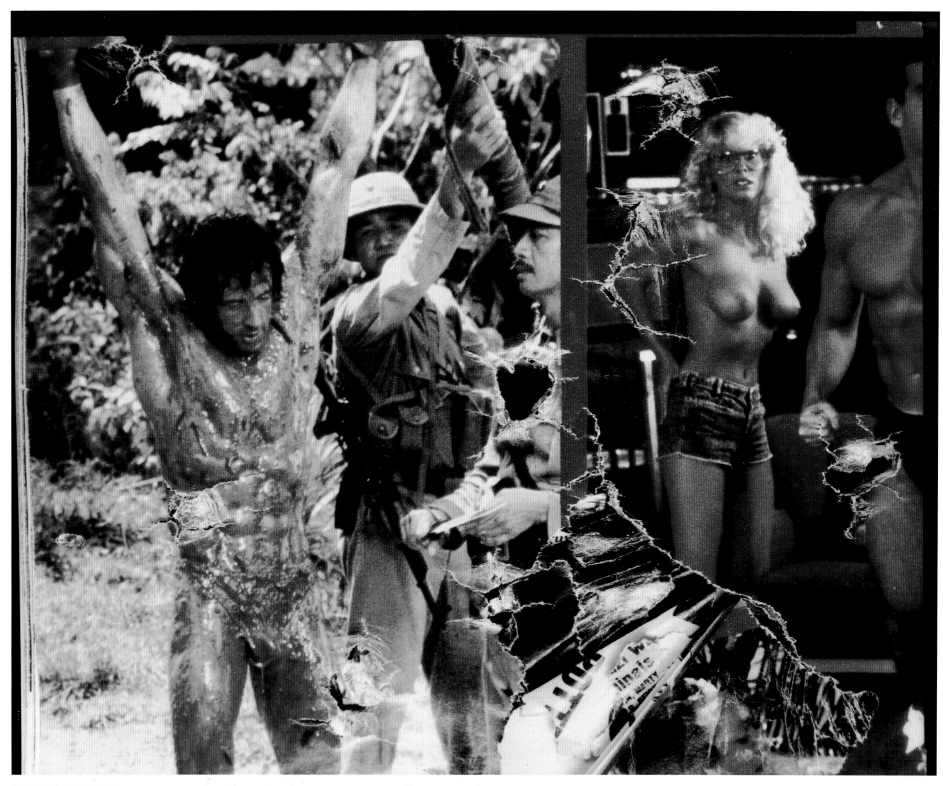

PLAYBOY #42 (RAMBO)

postscript:
an interview with richard misrach

(The following interview was edited from a tape-recorded conversation between Melissa Harris and Richard Misrach at his California studio in March 1992.)

Melissa Harris: How does *Violent Legacies* fit into your ongoing "Desert Cantos" project?

Richard Misrach: I began the "Desert Cantos" project around 1979. For over a decade, I have been searching the deserts of the American West for images that suggest the collision between "civilization" and nature. The three cantos that make up *Violent Legacies* are part of this larger project, but deal specifically with militarism and cultural violence.

The "canto" idea is actually very simple. It's a structural term meaning the subsection of a long song or poem. Throughout the history of literature it has been repeatedly used. Most people are familiar with Ezra Pound's epic poem, *The Cantos*, or Dante's *Inferno*, which is subdivided into cantos.

I found that, photographically, my work in the desert naturally broke into subseries. Each subseries, or canto, was independent, but related to the others. Combining the cantos created an epic, comprehensive relationship. Now I'm on "Desert Canto XIV."

I tend to work on several cantos simultaneously. I give them numbers upon completion, instead of when they are initiated, because they can change significantly as they evolve. The three cantos that comprise *Violent Legacies* are: "Desert Canto IX: Project W-47 (The Secret)"; "Desert Canto VI: The Pit"; and "Desert Canto XI: The Playboys."

Thus far, there are fourteen fully defined cantos (although some are still in progress) and a prologue. From one to fourteen, the cantos are: "The Terrain"; "The Event"; "The Flood"; "The Fires"; "The War (Bravo 20)"; "The Pit"; "Desert Seas"; "The Event II"; "Project W-47 (The Secret)"; "The Test Site"; "The Playboys"; "Clouds (non-equivalents)"; "The Inhabitants"; and "The Visitors."

M.H.: I know that some of your pre-cantos work was also done in the desert. There was a whole series of night desert landscapes of cacti and palm trees that were made in the mid seventies. What is it about the desert that holds such a fascination for you?

R.M.: I am not certain what it is that makes it so compelling. It does seem that the severity of the landscape sets cultural artifacts off in dramatic relief. The paucity of life there—in comparison with other environments, like forests and cities—is a reminder of how fragile human existence is. The desert has always provided rich material for literature and the visual arts, from the Bible to science-fiction films, probably because it epitomizes the extremes of the human condition.

And the deserts of the American West are particularly interesting because of their role in determining a peculiarly American identity and mythology. But I don't think I could have sustained this project for as long as I have if I didn't enjoy the process of working in the desert so much. It's the heat, the feel of the earth, the rich solitude and silence, and the remarkable scale of everything that makes being there so deeply fulfilling. I've always had this strange sensation of being a small figure in a vast landscape—as if I were seeing myself from the air. My best ideas seem to come when I'm driving those long stretches of desert highway. Physically and mentally, that's where I feel the most alive.

M.H.: Tell me about "Project W-47": the activities at Wendover, Utah, during World War II, its involvement with the atomic bomb, all the secrecy....

R.M.: During World War II, Wendover was a small desert town—population of approximately one hundred—with an existing army air base. Remotely

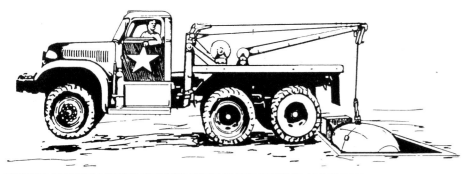

THE FRONT WHEELS OF THE WRECKER LEAVING THE GROUND AS A FAT MAN UNIT IS BEING LOWERED INTO THE LOADING PIT.

situated on the Nevada-Utah border, a hundred miles from the closest major city, Wendover was selected for the dangerous and top-secret final modification, assembly, and flight testing of the atomic bomb. Code-named

"Project W-47," the mission at Wendover was to turn the unwieldy atomic device, successfully detonated for the first time in July 1945 at Alamogordo, into a deliverable bomb.

It was at Wendover that the last-minute crucial details were worked out. For example, there was not enough clearance to load the huge bombs into the belly of a converted B-29 bomber by conventional means. So the bombs were set on a hydraulic lift inside a specially created cement pit. The plane would roll over the pit, and then the bomb would be carefully pushed into the plane's belly. Another important activity at Wendover was flight training. The heavy bombs had unusual flight characteristics, and the pilots and crews practiced bombing runs by flying from Wendover to drop dummy bombs (pumpkins) in the Salton Sea in California.

Without these efforts, the war would have continued with a massive land invasion of Japan. And the nuclear age as we know it might never have been initiated.

M.H.: You indicate that Wendover's role in the war remains a secret. Why is that? Certainly there are other programs of greater drama that are known about in detail. It seems like such a minor program—at least relatively speaking. After forty-five years, why has it remained a secret?

R.M.: That's a good question, and I don't know that I have an answer. James Rowe, the W-47 project commander at Wendover, has been trying to get recognition for his men's efforts, and implies that there are internal politics involved—that other bases got the credit due Wendover. However, there are others who believe that maybe more went on at Wendover than meets the eye. For example, there is the contention that there was a third atomic bomb that was en route to Japan and somehow got lost at sea. Interestingly, I pursued this matter myself, and after being bounced around from one military and government agency to another—almost everyone denying the existence of Project W-47—I talked to a military officer/historian who has been researching Wendover's history. Despite extremely high security clearance, even he was denied access to the Project W-47 files stored at Los Alamos. What could possibly be worth hiding at this date is hard to imagine.

But the details of Wendover are less important than what it symbolizes.

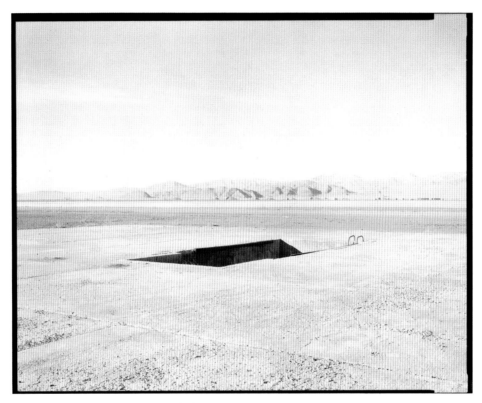

ATOMIC BOMB LOADING PIT

Wendover is an example of over 3,000 sites throughout the United States where secret military programs continue to this day. The military takes over vast tracts of remote land as well as urban sites; it experiments with weapons of mass destruction; and it maintains secrecy in the name of national security, when in actuality it is trying to keep the public from finding out about dangerous and unjustifiable programs.

Today, the Wendover base has been turned into a civilian airport, periodically reactivated for air-combat training. When I photographed there, between 1986 and 1991, I discovered historical traces and details that betrayed its concealed past. What still remains are the ammunition bunkers and bomber hangars, the dilapidated clapboard buildings and foundations, the runways and atomic-bomb pits, and telling signage and military graffiti.

M.H.: Let's turn to the second canto in *Violent Legacies*, entitled "The Pit." This may be the most difficult, and it is certainly the most graphic series in the book. First off, how did you come across it?

R.M.: A poet who lived on the Stillwater Indian reservation in Nevada told me about the pits of dead animals. He was aware of my work, and described this Bosch-like landscape that I had to see. He told me to drive out to the general vicinity and to watch for the crows. I sat out there for a day, but nothing happened. I had practically given up when, suddenly, dozens of crows lifted off from the middle of nowhere. I couldn't believe it. I located a dirt trail heading in that direction, climbed a ridge and there it was, the hideous spectacle. Hundreds of animals were piled together in a surreal, fraternal death embrace. That was in 1987.

M.H.: In this series, the text that accompanies the pictures is a historical account of a fallout incident from the 1950s, but the photographs were made in the 1980s. Therefore, the animals depicted are clearly not the animals affected by the 1953 atomic test. Why have you paired the two?

R.M.: Before I learned about the pits, I had just read declassified accounts of the atrocities of our atomic-testing program, and was horrified and outraged. Even though the accounts were now in the public domain, I realized that, without visual documentation, the written records seemed to make little impact. When I saw the dead animals, it brought to mind the 1953 incident. I felt that combining the earlier account with the graphic images would be a viable way of creating a generic protest of our military and government contamination of the environment and the inevitable cover-ups. You have to realize that the accident at Chernobyl in 1986 was still very fresh in everyone's mind, and made clear that the atrocities of nuclear testing were not confined to the forties and fifties, but in fact continue into the present.

When I first began photographing at the pits (there were three altogether), I was led to understand that they were not an unusual phenomenon, as bizarre as they appeared to a city boy. Depository sites for dead animals, like trash dumps, were common in the West. Later on, however, I discovered a string of coincidences that raised suspicion about the particular sites I was concentrating on, and about why the animals there were dying in such numbers. There was one atomic test in the Fallon area in 1963 (Operation Shoal) that is rumored to have created hot spots of plutonium and high rates of leukemia. Then, around 1990, an internal study of Naval Air Station Fallon indicated that twenty highly toxic pits on the base were leaching into the water table and threatening local agriculture and livestock. The base pits are contaminated with a range of hazardous materials, from jet fuel and PCBs to napalm. The animal pits are now being investigated.

M.H.: Is the investigation based on your photographs?

R.M.: Yes. An agent from the Bureau of Land Management became concerned upon seeing the photographs in "The Pit" series and contacted the Bureau of Reclamation. Apparently, something in the photographs sent up a red flag. They've initiated an investigation and promised to keep me informed. As of this interview, I'm still waiting to hear.

If the photographs can actually help affect a specific site, that would be great. More important, however, we have to recognize that the military and governmental policies that have created nuclear and other kinds of toxic contamination and kept them secret continue today, everywhere. They're not confined to Churchill County or the Sand Springs Valley, but are literally global in scope.

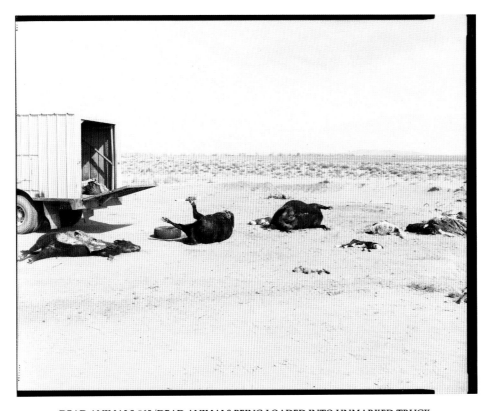

DEAD ANIMALS #65 (DEAD ANIMALS BEING LOADED INTO UNMARKED TRUCK
DESTINED FOR RENO RENDERING PLANT. ACCORDING TO THE DRIVER, THE
ANIMAL CORPSES WERE TO BE CONVERTED INTO DOG FOOD AND OATMEAL.)

M.H.: Finally, "The Playboys." Obviously, this canto looks different from the rest. How does it fit in with the "Desert Cantos" in general, and specifically with *Violent Legacies*?

R.M.: The "Desert Cantos" project is built around the found metaphor. The discovery of the shot-up *Playboy* magazines fits in perfectly. South of Tonopah, near the northwest corner of the Nuclear Test Site in Nevada, lies a typical desert target range used by locals. The landscape is littered with the predictable detritus—spent shells, broken glass, and pulverized cans. On one of my visits, in 1988, I discovered the two magazines. One was propped against a shot-up television, the other was half-buried in the dirt. As usual, I photographed the scene as I found it. While I was maneuvering for a good angle, a breeze blew open the magazine to a picture of Ray Charles singing for Memorex. His Memorex ecstasy was transformed into a scream by a bullet that had ripped through the magazine. I realized that the women on the covers of both magazines were the intended targets, but that in the bullet's passage though the remaining pages, other symbols of our culture were randomly violated, too. The violence that was directed specifically at the women symbolically penetrated every layer of our society. (Somebody, I wish I could remember who, said, in effect, that *Playboy* magazine is the encyclopedia of American culture.) Every aspect of our society—gender, race, class, the environment, even language itself—was riddled with violence.

I decided to take the magazines with me, and initially exhibited them in a gallery as found objects. Every few days, the gallery attendant opened the *Playboys* randomly to a new spread. For me, they were the pivotal pieces in an exhibition addressing cultural violence. Remarkably, the reviews and extensive exhibition catalog didn't even mention the magazines. I was stunned. It was then that I decided to rephotograph them—selecting individual pages and spreads—and to make large prints. The exaggerated scale and object quality released their metaphorical potency. Despite the fact that they were just pieces of paper, pictures with holes in them, the gashed representations elicited a powerful and uncanny visceral response.

M.H.: The work in *Violent Legacies* is tough and disturbing, yet it does not seem to be apocalyptic. Is there hope or redemption in your work?

R.M.: I confess to being an incorrigible romantic and I believe that art is a vital force in the shaping of reality. The "redemptive" qualities of dark poetry lie in an ability to rupture existing myths and paradigms. For example, *Violent Legacies* portrays a Western landscape that is very different from the stereotypes that have become synonymous with the American identity. The West is symbolized by the heroic white male, riding on horseback with a gun on his hip, taking on all threats and obstacles, surviving and conquering the wilderness, Indians, and so on. Despite its obvious historical shortfalls, and its laughable lack of any resemblance to life in the West in the 1990s, this still functions as an extremely potent cultural myth. Interestingly, the myth of the cowboy seems to be directly derived from another powerful mythological figure: Homer's Odysseus.

The pictures in *Violent Legacies* are an attempt to provide an alternative, more accurate way of understanding the West. They show a land not of open spaces and wilderness—of loners subsisting on the earth's natural bounty, and heroic efforts to "civilize" the West—but a land used by military and government agencies for the development of weapons of mass destruction ("Project W-47"), a land where natural resources are poisoned ("The Pit"), and where symbolic acts of violence with a gun portray a culture gone berserk ("The Playboys"). Maybe a more accurate myth of today's West would be that of Frankenstein. The landscape has become a laboratory where scientists experiment with the powers of the universe—chemical, biological, electronic, and nuclear—leading to dangerous creations that are impossible to control.

We have become a drastically militarized society, and yet we seem to be unaware of this fact. In the meantime, the military is devouring our resources and talent, destroying the environment, and providing violent models for conflict resolution on both national and individual levels.

M.H.: What are the relationships among your artistic intentions, your political activism, and your evident desire to uncover truths? Is your work journalistic documentation? Is it about aesthetics? Or is it a sort of hybrid?

R.M.: First off, all art reflects one's politics, whether consciously or otherwise. Certainly, some images are more overtly political than others. Sometimes the politics are layered, problematic, and very complex. Being a

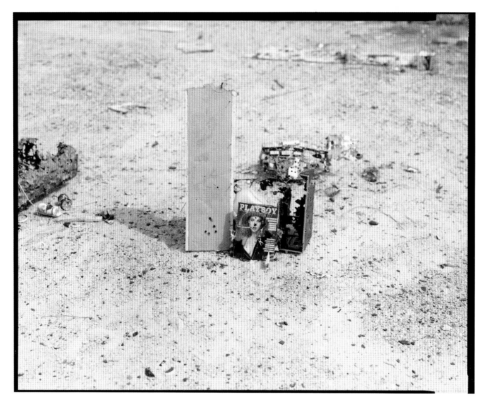

PLAYBOY MAGAZINE AS FOUND ON SITE, 1988

white, male, American artist affects or skews my perspective on everything I do from the outset. The best I can do is try to keep this self-consciousness at the forefront while I work, and not assume that the "truths" I discover are objective or universal.

The very act of representation has been so thoroughly challenged in recent years by postmodern theories that it is impossible not to see the flaws everywhere, in any practice of photography. Traditional genres in particular—journalism, documentary studies, and fine-art photography— have become shells, or forms emptied of meaning. Victor Burgin underscored a significant point when he made the distinction between the "representation of politics" and the "politics of representation." Nonetheless, despite the limitations and problems inherent to photographic representation (and especially the representation of politics), it remains for me the most powerful and engaging medium today—one central to the development of cultural dialogue.

The "Desert Cantos" project of the last decade has shifted somewhat in the nature of its representation. The earliest series, "The Terrain," "The Event," "The Flood," and "The Fires," for example, were more or less aesthetic metaphors. Recent cantos, however, have become more explicitly political. The "Bravo 20" project points a finger directly at military abuse of the environment. I think the three cantos in *Violent Legacies* hover between the two.

M.H.: Richard, your photographs are visually very seductive. Yet your subjects are death, contamination, and violence. Are you perhaps aestheticizing the horrific, and thus exploiting it?

R.M.: Probably the strongest criticism leveled at my work is that I'm making "poetry of the holocaust." But I've come to believe that beauty can be a very powerful conveyor of difficult ideas. It engages people when they might otherwise look away.

Recent theory has been critical of the distancing effect of artistic expression—"Create solutions, not art." But the impact of art may be more complex and far-reaching than theory is capable of assessing. To me, the work I do is a means of interpreting unsettling truths, of bearing witness, and of sounding an alarm. The beauty of formal representation both carries an affirmation of life and subversively brings us face to face with news from our besieged world.

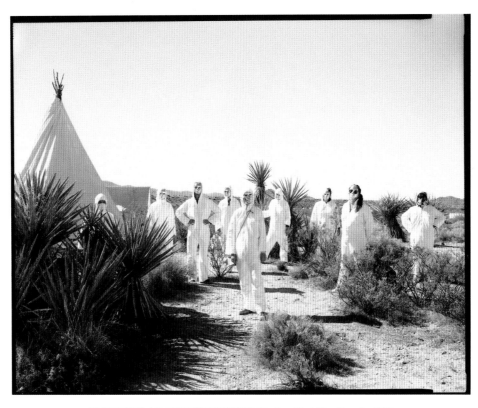

PRINCESSES AGAINST PLUTONIUM, Nuclear Test Site, Nevada, 1988

IN APRIL OF 1988, NINE WOMEN CALLING THEMSELVES THE PRINCESSES OF
PLUTONIUM HIKED UNDETECTED ACROSS THE DESERT INTO THE NATION'S
NUCLEAR TESTING GROUNDS. AT DAWN, DRESSED IN RADIATION SUITS
AND DEATH MASKS, THE PRINCESSES HANDED OUT FLIERS TO THE INCOMING
WORKERS STATING THAT "THE AREA IS CONTAMINATED, EVACUATE
IMMEDIATELY." THE WOMEN WERE ARRESTED AND FACED A POSSIBLE SIX-
MONTH JAIL SENTENCE. THEIR PERFORMANCE, HOWEVER, INSPIRED
HUNDREDS OF "COPYCAT" INVASIONS AND ARRESTS, WHICH JAMMED THE
COURTS AND ULTIMATELY RESULTED IN THE CHARGES AGAINST THE
PRINCESSES BEING DISMISSED.

acknowledgments

First and foremost, I wish to acknowledge my wife Myriam Weisang Misrach for her love and brilliance, and my son Jacob Bloomfield-Misrach for his love and generosity of heart. What joy and strength they have brought to my life.

Susan Sontag's fiction provides an important framework for the *Violent Legacies* project. I am thrilled by her participation.

For their aid and contributions in research I would like to thank Bill Wolfington, Brent Jones, James Rowe, Bob Fulkerson and Grace Bukowski of Citizen Alert, Kirk Robertson, Bill Rosse, and for sheer inspiration, Rachel Johnson and the Princesses of Plutonium.

This project was partially supported by a Eureka Fellowship from the Fleishacker Foundation, for which I am extremely grateful.

For their support and friendship thanks go to: Dr. Richard Bargen, Frish Brandt, James Danziger, Penny Dolginer, Catherine Edelman, Terry Etherton, Jeff Fraenkel, Sy Fuhrman, Gail Gibson, Ursula Gropper, Lisa Hyde, Leslie Hyde, Bill Kaufman, Jan Kesner, Tom Meyer, Theresa Luisotti, Maya Ishiwata, Bob Mann, Maria Marewski, Anita Misrach, Rebecca Solnit, and Barry and Elyse Weinstein.

For superb reproduction and exhibition prints, I would like to acknowledge the work of Linda Potts of Imagechrome, Inc., and more recently, the crew at Custom Process Lab, including Howard Brainen, Bob Ditmanson, Jacqueline Reynolds, Kerry Stamps, Rafia Syed, and in particular the exceptional printing of Jill Haley.

Finally, thanks go to my editor Melissa Harris for bringing the project to Aperture and overseeing its painstaking execution. I would also like to thank the unheralded staff at Aperture, particularly Michael Sand and Stevan Baron. Roger Gorman's creative design work was a constant delight. A difficult book such as this would not exist if it were not for the unwavering commitment of Michael Hoffman.

— Richard Misrach

Aperture gratefully acknowledges the generous support of: The Andy Warhol Foundation for the Visual Arts, Inc., and the Lynne and Harold Honickman Foundation.

Our special thanks to *Playboy* for their cooperation.

Book and jacket design by Roger Gorman. Composition by Leah Sherman/Betty Type, Inc.

Printed and bound in Italy by Sfera/Officine Grafiche Garzanti Editore S.p.A.

Color separations by Sfera, Milan, Italy.

The staff at Aperture for *Violent Legacies: Three Cantos* is Michael E. Hoffman, Executive Director; Melissa Harris, Editor; Michael Sand, Managing Editor; Suzan Sherman, Annie Wiesenthal, Editorial Work-Scholars; Stevan Baron, Production Director; Sandra Greve, Production Associate.

Aperture publishes a periodical, books, and portfolios of fine photography to communicate with serious photographers and creative people everywhere. A complete catalog is available upon request. Address: 20 East 23rd Street, New York, New York 10010.

First edition
10 9 8 7 6 5 4 3 2 1